2017 SUPPLEMENT TO

CONSTITUTIONAL LAW

CASES, COMMENTS, AND QUESTIONS

Twelfth Edition

■ ■ ■

Jesse H. Choper
Earl Warren Professor of Public Law,
University of California, Berkeley

Richard H. Fallon, Jr.
Story Professor of Law,
Harvard University

Yale Kamisar
Distinguished Professor of Law, University of San Diego
Clarence Darrow Distinguished University Professor Emeritus of Law,
University of Michigan

Steven H. Shiffrin
Charles Frank Reavis, Sr., Professor of Law,
Cornell University

Michael C. Dorf
Robert S. Stevens Professor of Law,
Cornell University

Frederick Schauer
David and Mary Harrison Distinguished Professor of Law,
University of Virginia

AMERICAN CASEBOOK SERIES®

WEST ACADEMIC PUBLISHING

American Casebook Series is a trademark registered in the U.S. Patent and Trademark Office.

© 2015, 2016 LEG, Inc. d/b/a West Academic
© 2017 LEG, Inc. d/b/a West Academic
    444 Cedar Street, Suite 700
    St. Paul, MN 55101
    1-877-888-1330

West, West Academic Publishing, and West Academic are trademarks of West Publishing Corporation, used under license.

Printed in the United States of America

ISBN: 978-1-68328-713-1

TABLE OF CONTENTS

TABLE OF CASES

The principal cases are in bold type.

———————

TABLE OF AUTHORITIES

2017 SUPPLEMENT TO

CONSTITUTIONAL LAW

CASES, COMMENTS, AND QUESTIONS

Twelfth Edition

CHAPTER 2

NATIONAL LEGISLATIVE POWER

■ ■ ■

2. THE NATIONAL COMMERCE POWER

IV. NEW LIMITATIONS IN THE 21st CENTURY

P. 127, add fn. 61a at the end of the opinion:

[61a] In *Taylor v. United States*, the Court, in an opinion by Alito, J., applied *Raich* to construe the jurisdictional element of a federal statute that was deemed to reach to the full extent of the Commerce power. "In order to obtain a conviction under the Hobbs Act for the robbery or attempted robbery of a drug dealer," the Court wrote, "the Government need not show that the drugs that a defendant stole or attempted to steal either traveled or were destined for transport across state lines." Thomas, J., dissented on the ground that the ruling "extends our already expansive, flawed commerce-power precedents."

CHAPTER 3

DISTRIBUTION OF FEDERAL POWERS: SEPARATION OF POWERS

■ ■ ■

1. PRESIDENTIAL ACTION AFFECTING "CONGRESSIONAL" POWERS

II. EXTERNAL MATTERS: FOREIGN AFFAIRS AND WAR

P. 205, before *Campbell*:

ZIVOTOFSKY v. KERRY, 135 S.Ct. 2076 (2015), per KENNEDY, J., held that an act of Congress [§ 214(d)], requiring the Secretary of State to allow citizens born in Jerusalem to list their place of birth as 'Israel' on passports, "directly contradicts [the] carefully calibrated and longstanding Executive branch policy of neutrality toward Jerusalem," thus interfering with the President's "exclusive power to grant formal recognition to a foreign sovereign," as shown by the "Constitution's text and structure, as well as precedent and history":

"It is a logical and proper inference" that the "Reception Clause, which directs that the President 'shall receive Ambassadors and other public Ministers,' Art. II, § 3, [should] be understood to acknowledge his power to recognize other nations." In addition, Art. II, § 2, cl. 2 provides that the President "shall nominate * * * Ambassadors as well as 'other public Ministers and Consuls.'" This includes "dispatch[ing] other diplomatic agents [and] engaging in direct diplomacy with foreign heads of state and their ministers." The power that "the President may unilaterally effect recognition—and the lack of any similar power vested in Congress—[as well] as "functional considerations, suggest [that] the Nation must have a single policy regarding which governments are legitimate in the eyes of the United States." Thus, "the President since the founding has exercised this unilateral power to recognize new states—and the Court has endorsed the practice," citing *Pink, Belmont,* and *Banco Nacional de Cuba v. Sabbatino*, 376 U.S. 398 (1964) (status of Cuba's Government and its acts as a sovereign), all illustrating that "the Court has long considered recognition to be the exclusive prerogative of the Executive [and] the sole organ of the federal government in the field of international relations. [To] be effective in negotiations over a formal recognition determination, it must be evident to his counterparts abroad that he speaks for the Nation on that precise question." Nor does *Curtiss-Wright* indicate that

3

"the Executive is not free from the ordinary controls and checks of Congress merely because foreign affairs are at issue.

"[H]istory is not all on one side, but on balance it provides strong support for the conclusion that the recognition power is the President's alone, [establishing] no more than that some Presidents have chosen to ["consult and coordinate"] with Congress, not that Congress itself has exercised the recognition power."

Finally, "the subject is quite narrow: The Executive's exclusive power extends no further than his formal recognition determination. [This] is not to say Congress may not express its disagreement with the President in myriad ways. For example, it may enact an embargo, decline to confirm an ambassador, or even declare war. But none of these acts would alter the President's recognition decision."[1]

Thomas, J., concurred in the judgment in part and dissented in part. "Our Constitution vests the residual foreign affairs powers of the Federal Government—i.e., those not specifically enumerated in the Constitution—in the President by way of Article II's Vesting Clause. [It] includes all powers originally understood as falling within the 'executive power' of the Federal Government. [The] President has long regulated passports under his residual foreign affairs power, [preceded "in England, by the King; in the colonies, by the Continental Congress; and in the United States, by President Washington and every President since,"] and this portion of § 214(d) does not fall within any of Congress' enumerated powers. By contrast, § 214(d) poses no such problem insofar as it regulates consular reports of birth abroad.[2] [These] were ["historically associated with" and] were developed to effectuate the naturalization laws, [and fall] within Congress' enumerated powers under the Naturalization and Necessary and Proper Clauses.[3] [The] Court relies on a distortion of the President's recognition power to hold both of these parts of § 214(d) unconstitutional. [Assuming] for the sake of argument that listing a nonrecognized foreign sovereign as a citizen's place of birth on a U.S. passport could have the effect of recognizing that sovereign under international law, no such recognition would occur [here]. The United States has recognized Israel as a foreign sovereign since May 14, 1948. That the United States has subsequently declined to acknowledge Israel's sovereignty over Jerusalem has not changed its recognition of Israel as a sovereign state. * * *

I concur only in the portion of the Court's judgment holding § 214(d) unconstitutional as applied to passports. I respectfully dissent from the remainder."[4]

---

[1] Breyer, J., joined the Court's opinion but added "that this case presents a political question. See *Zivotofsky v. Clinton*," Ch. 1 Sec. 2 of the Casebook.

[2] Since petitioners waived this issue, it was not considered by the Court.

[3] For fuller discussion of Thomas, J.'s position, see his opinions in *Comstock* and *Morrison*, Ch. 2 of the Casebook, text at fns. 17 and 54.

[4] For Thomas, J.'s response to Scalia, J.'s criticism of his opinion, see fn. 5.

Scalia, J., joined by Roberts, C.J. and Alito, J., dissented: "One would think that if Congress may grant Zivotofsky a passport and a birth report [under its naturalization power], it may also require these papers to record his birthplace as 'Israel.' [W]hen faced with alternative ways to carry its powers into execution, Congress has the 'discretion' to choose the one it deems 'most beneficial to the people,' *McCulloch*, [and] thus has the right to decide that recording birthplaces as 'Israel' makes for better foreign policy. Or that regardless of international politics, a passport or birth report should respect its bearer's conscientious belief that Jerusalem belongs to Israel.

" * * * I agree that the Constitution *empowers* the President to extend recognition on behalf of the United States, but I find it a much harder question whether it makes that power exclusive. [In any event,] § 214(d) plainly does not concern recognition [which]is a formal legal act with effects under international law. [M]aking a notation in a passport or birth report does not encumber the Republic with any international obligations. * * *

"The best indication that § 214(d) does not concern recognition comes from the State Department's policies concerning Taiwan. [T]he United States 'acknowledges the Chinese position' that Taiwan is a part of China, but 'does not take a position' of its own on that issue. Even so, the State Department has for a long time recorded the birthplace of a citizen born in Taiwan as 'China' [until] Congress passed a law (on which § 214(d) was modeled) giving citizens the option to have their birthplaces recorded as 'Taiwan.' [Section] 214(d) likewise calls for nothing beyond a 'geographic description'; it does not require the Executive even to assert, never mind formally recognize, that Jerusalem is a part of sovereign Israel.

"[§ 214(d) shows] only that the law displays symbolic support for Israel's territorial claim. That symbolism may have tremendous significance as a matter of international diplomacy, but it makes no difference as a matter of constitutional law. Even if the Constitution gives the President sole power to extend recognition, it does not give him sole power to make all decisions relating to foreign disputes over sovereignty. To the contrary, a fair reading of Article I's [power] to "regulate Commerce with foreign Nations," § 8, cl. 3, includes power to regulate imports from Gibraltar as British goods or as Spanish goods. * * *

"It would be comical to claim [that § 214(d)] interferes with the President's ability to withhold recognition. [The] Court identifies no reason to believe that the United States—or indeed any other country—uses the place-of-birth field in passports and birth reports as a forum for performing the act of recognition. [To] the extent doubts linger, § 214(d) leaves the President free to dispel them by issuing a disclaimer of intent to recognize. A disclaimer always suffices to prevent an act from effecting recognition.

"[There] is no question that Congress may, if it wishes, pass laws that openly flout treaties made by the President. [Today's] holding puts the implied power to recognize territorial claims (which the Court infers from the power to recognize states, which it infers from the responsibility to receive ambassadors) on a higher footing than the express power to make treaties.

"In the end, the Court's decision does not rest on text or history or precedent. It instead comes down to 'functional considerations'—principally the Court's perception that the Nation 'must speak with one voice' about the status of Jerusalem. * * * Functionalism of the sort the Court practices today will *systematically* favor the unitary President over the plural Congress in disputes involving foreign affairs. It is possible that this approach will make for more effective foreign policy, perhaps as effective as that of a monarchy. It is certain that, in the long run, it will erode the structure of separated powers that the People established for the protection of their liberty.

"Justice Thomas's concurrence [finds] no congressional power that would extend to the issuance or contents of passports. Including the power to regulate foreign commerce [and five other powers.] The concurrence's stingy interpretation of the enumerated powers forgets that the Constitution does not 'partake of the prolixity of a legal code.' [Contrary to Thomas, J.'s view, the power to control passports was not exclusive to the executive in either England or the United States.] This Court has held that the President may not curtail a citizen's travel by withholding a passport, *except on grounds approved by Congress. Kent* v. *Dulles.* History and precedent thus refute any suggestion that the Constitution disables Congress from regulating the President's issuance and formulation of passports.

"[Finally, Thomas, J., suggests] that *even if* Congress's enumerated powers otherwise encompass § 214(d), and *even if* the President's power to regulate the contents of passports is not exclusive, the law might *still* violate the Constitution, because it 'conflict[s]' with the President's passport policy. It turns the Constitution upside-down to suggest that in areas of shared authority, it is the executive policy that preempts the law, rather than the other way around. Congress *may* make laws necessary and proper for carrying into execution the President's powers, Art. I, § 8, cl. 18, but the President *must* 'take Care' that Congress's legislation 'be faithfully executed,' Art. II, § 3. And Acts of Congress made in pursuance of the Constitution are the 'supreme Law of the Land'; acts of the President (apart from treaties) are not.[5]

Roberts, C.J., joined by Alito, J., filed a separate dissent: "Never before has this Court accepted a President's direct defiance of an Act of Congress in the field of foreign affairs. We have instead stressed that the President's power reaches 'its lowest ebb' when he contravenes the express will of Congress [*Youngstown* (Jackson, J., concurring.) The] President claims the exclusive and preclusive power to recognize foreign sovereigns. The Court devotes much of its analysis to accepting the Executive's contention. I have serious doubts about that position. [At] the founding, "there was no reason to view the

---

[5]   Thomas, J.'s response mainly argued that (1) Scalia, J., did not adequately "confront difficult questions about the application of the Necessary and proper Clause in the case of conflict among the branches," and (2) "although the consular report of birth abroad shares some features with a passport, it is historically associated with naturalization, not foreign affairs."

reception clause as a source of discretionary authority for the president." Adler, *The President's Recognition Power: Ministerial or Discretionary?* 25 Presidential Studies Q. 267 (1995). * * *

"[E]ven if the President does have exclusive recognition power, he still cannot prevail in this case, because the statute at issue *does not implicate recognition*. [N]either Congress nor the Executive Branch regards § 214(d) as a recognition determination. * * *

"If the President's so-called general foreign relations authority does not permit him to countermand a State's lawful action [*Medellin*], it surely does not authorize him to disregard an express statutory directive enacted by Congress, which—unlike the States—has extensive foreign relations powers of its own."

2. CONGRESSIONAL ACTION AFFECTING "PRESIDENTIAL" POWERS

III. APPOINTMENT AND REMOVAL OF OFFICERS

P. 262, before Sec. 3:

NLRB v. CANNING, 134 S.Ct. 2558 (2014), per BREYER, J., held that President Obama's "appointment of three of the Board's five members, during a 3-day 'pro-forma' recess of the Senate," was invalid under the Appointments Clause, which allows for recess appointments "so that the President can ensure the continued functioning of the Federal Government when the Senate is away": Under "the longstanding 'practice of the government' *McCulloch*, [the] phrase 'the recess' includes an intra-session recess of substantial length." * * *

"History also offers strong support. [Since 1929,] Congress has shortened its inter-session breaks as it has taken longer and more frequent intra-session breaks; Presidents have correspondingly [made] thousands of intra-session recess appointments. [We] think the Framers likely did intend the Clause to apply to a new circumstance that so clearly falls within its essential purposes, where doing so is consistent with the Clauses's language. [T]he most likely reason the Framers did not place a textual floor underneath the word 'recess' is that they did not foresee the *need* for one. [And] they might not have anticipated that intra-session recesses would become lengthier and more significant than inter-session [ones. As to] how long a recess must be in order to fall within the Clause, [we] conclude, in light of historical practice, that a recess of more than 3 days but less than 10 days is presumptively too short to fall within the Clause. We add the word 'presumptively' to leave open the possibility that some very unusual circumstance—a national catastrophe, for instance, that renders the Senate unavailable but calls for an urgent response—could demand the exercise of the recess-appointment power during a shorter break.

"[As to] the scope of the phrase 'vacancies *that may happen* during the recess of the Senate,' [all] agree that the phrase applies to vacancies that initially occur during a recess. But does it also 'apply to vacancies that initially occur before a recess and continue to exist during the recess? In our view the phrase applies to both kinds of vacancy [because its] purpose is to permit the President to obtain the assistance of subordinate officers when the Senate, due to its recess, cannot confirm [them.] Historical practice over the past 200 years strongly favors the broader interpretation [as] Presidents since Madison have made many recess appointments filling vacancies that initially occurred prior to a recess."

As for "calculation of the length of the Senate's 'recess,' [the] President made the recess appointments before us on January 4, 2012, in between the January 3 and the January 6 pro forma sessions. [W]e conclude that when the Senate declares that it is in session and possesses the capacity, under its own rules, to conduct business, it is in session for purposes of the Clause [and] Senate rules make clear that, once in session, the Senate can act even if it has earlier said that it would not."

Since the appointments in the case were during a recess of only three days, they were not within the President's authority.

SCALIA, J., joined by Roberts, C.J., and Thomas and Alito, JJ., concurred in the judgment but submitted a long, detailed disagreement, qualifying or contradicting the Court's rationale point by point. He emphasized "the folly of interpreting constitutional provisions designed to establish 'a structure of government that would protect liberty,' *Bowsher*, on the narrow-minded assumption that their only purpose is to make the government run as efficiently as possible."

As a matter of both "plain meaning [and] historical practice," (1) Recess is "the gap between sessions and [the] appointments at issue here are invalid because they undisputedly were made during the Senate's session;" and] (2) "vacancies" are those "that arise during the recess in which they are filled."

CHAPTER 4

STATE POWER TO REGULATE

■ ■ ■

5. STATE POWER TO TAX

P. 360, after note 3(c):

4. ***Internal consistency and a state's taxation of its own citizens.***
COMPTROLLER OF THE TREASURY OF MARYLAND v. WYNNE, 135 S.Ct.
1787 (2015), invalidated a Maryland tax scheme under which Maryland
residents were taxed on income earned both in Maryland and in other states
but did not receive a full Maryland tax credit for taxes paid to other states on
out-of-state income. Writing for the Court, ALITO, J., held that Maryland's
denial of a full credit for taxes paid to other stats failed the "internal
consistency" test under which a tax violates the dormant Commerce Clause if
its hypothetical adoption by all states would interfere with interstate
commerce: if every state taxed on the same basis as Maryland, income
generated in interstate commerce would be taxed at a higher rate (because it
would be taxed by more than one state) than that earned in intrastate
commerce. GINSBURG, J., joined by Scalia and Kagan, JJ., dissented on the
grounds that the Maryland tax scheme was "evenhanded" because it taxed
residents' income the same whether earned in-state or out-of-state and that
the political process adequately safeguards against abuse of state authority in
imposing evenhanded taxes. Scalia, J., and Thomas, J., also dissented.

CHAPTER 5

SUBSTANTIVE PROTECTION OF ECONOMIC INTERESTS

■ ■ ■

4. OTHER LIMITS ON ECONOMIC LEGISLATION: THE PROHIBITION AGAINST "TAKING" "PRIVATE PROPERTY" WITHOUT JUST COMPENSATION

P. 401, after the first full paragraph:

The Court applied *Loretto* in HORNE v. DEP'T OF AGRICULTURE, 135 S.Ct. 2419 (2015). Under the authority of a federal statute enacted during the Great Depression, the Secretary of Agriculture ordered raisin growers to set aside a portion of their crop for the federal government to dispose as it saw fit, with net proceeds from government sales, if any, distributed to growers. The petitioners refused to comply with orders requiring the sacrifice of 47 percent of their raisins in one year and 30 percent in another, arguing that the program was a taking. The Court, per ROBERTS, C.J., agreed. Finding "[n]othing in th[e] history [of the Takings Clause to] suggest[] that personal property was any less protected against physical appropriation than real property," he deemed this "physical appropriation of personal property" subject to the *per se* rule of *Loretto*. The Court rejected the government's contention that the contingent right to receive compensation changed the character of the government program. The Court also rejected the government's characterization of the program as a condition on the privilege of selling raisins. "Selling produce in interstate commerce, although certainly subject to reasonable government regulation, is [not] a special governmental benefit that the Government may hold hostage, to be ransomed by the waiver of constitutional protection."

BREYER, J., joined by Ginsburg and Kagan, JJ., concurred in part and dissented in part. Although he agreed that the program was a taking, he would have remanded to the lower courts for a determination of the extent to which the benefits the program conferred on growers (chiefly in the form of higher raisin prices due to limited supply) offset the market value of the raisins that the petitioners were required to set aside. SOTOMAYOR, J., dissented on the ground that the *per se* rule of *Loretto* ought not to apply where the growers retained at least one "stick" in the bundle of property rights in their raisins, namely "the right to receive some money for the[ ] disposition" of the raisins reserved for the government.

———

P. 402, before final paragraph:

How to Determine the "Denominator" in Calculating Whether a Regulatory Taking Has Occurred?

To determine whether a regulation deprives an owner of all economically beneficial use of his or her property, courts must compare what is restricted against the whole. What is the whole? In *Penn Central*, the property owner argued that the regulation restricted all of the "air rights" above Grand Central Terminal, but the Court rejected that framing, treating the relevant parcel as encompassing the underlying land and building as well. In MURR v. WISCONSIN, 137 S.Ct. 1933 (2017), state and local law implementing a federally-imposed conservation mandate restricted development on certain lots with less than an acre of developable land, while also restricting the sale of adjacent lots under common ownership by merging them into one parcel. Members of the Murr family acquired two adjacent lots at different times and wanted to sell one of them to pay for development on the other, but were forbidden from doing so. They argued that each lot was a separate parcel for takings purposes and that the restrictions on one of the lots left them with no economically beneficial use of that lot. The Court, per KENNEDY, J., disagreed with the Murrs' characterization of the relevant parcel. Invoking the principle that the Takings Clause protects property owners' "reasonable expectations," the Court held that "no single consideration can supply the exclusive test for determining the denominator. Instead, courts must consider a number of factors. These include the treatment of the land under state and local law; the physical characteristics of the land; and the prospective value of the regulated land." Evaluating these factors, the Court concluded that the state "merger provision" was "a legitimate exercise of government power," and thus the relevant parcel comprised both lots. The composite parcel retained substantial economically beneficial use, so there was no *per se* taking under *Lucas*; and the "coordinated federal, state, and local effort to preserve [a] river and surrounding land" resulted in "a reasonable land-use regulation," so there was also no taking "under the more general test of *Penn Central*."

ROBERTS, C.J., joined by Thomas and Alito, JJ., dissented from the Court's multi-factor test on the ground that it led to "double counting" of the state's interest by first factoring in the reasonableness of the regulation in determining the proper parcel and then considering the regulation's reasonableness in applying *Penn Central*. The Chief Justice would have relied on state law alone to define each plot. In response to the majority's argument that the merger provision was part of state law, the dissent complained that it was a special rule created by the Wisconsin courts for regulatory takings cases, rather than an "ordinary principle[ ] of Wisconsin property law."

THOMAS, J., also dissented for himself alone, suggesting that in a future case the Court should "take a fresh look at our regulatory takings jurisprudence, to see whether it can be grounded in the original public meaning of the Takings Clause of the Fifth Amendment or the Privileges or Immunities Clause of the Fourteenth Amendment."

CHAPTER 6

PROTECTION OF INDIVIDUAL RIGHTS: DUE PROCESS, THE BILL OF RIGHTS, AND UNENUMERATED RIGHTS

■ ■ ■

2. THE RIGHT OF "PRIVACY" (OR "AUTONOMY")

P. 491, substitute for *Gonzales v. Carhart* and the Notes and Questions that follow on pages 491–500:

Purported Health Regulations

WHOLE WOMAN'S HEALTH V. HELLERSTEDT
___ U.S. ___,136 S.Ct. 2292, 195 L.Ed.2d 665 (2016).

JUSTICE BREYER delivered the opinion of the Court.

In *Planned Parenthood v. Casey,* a plurality of the Court concluded that there "exists" an "undue burden" on a woman's right to decide to have an abortion, and consequently a provision of law is constitutionally invalid, if the *"purpose or effect"* of the provision *"is to place a substantial obstacle in the path of a woman seeking an abortion before the fetus attains viability."* (Emphasis added.) The plurality added that "[u]nnecessary health regulations that have the purpose or effect of presenting a substantial obstacle to a woman seeking an abortion impose an undue burden on the right."

We must here decide whether two provisions of Texas' House Bill 2 violate the Federal Constitution as interpreted in *Casey.* The first provision, which we shall call the *"admitting-privileges requirement,"* says that "[a] physician performing or inducing an abortion . . . must, on the date the abortion is performed or induced, have active admitting privileges at a hospital that . . . is located not further than 30 miles from the location at which the abortion is performed or induced."

[The] second provision, which we shall call the *"surgical-center requirement,"* says that "the minimum standards for an abortion facility must be equivalent to the minimum standards adopted under [the Texas Health and Safety Code section] for ambulatory surgical centers."

We conclude that neither of these provisions offers medical benefits sufficient to justify the burdens upon access that each imposes. Each places a substantial obstacle in the path of women seeking a previability abortion, each constitutes an undue burden on abortion access and each violates the [Fourteenth Amendment].

I.   [B.] The District Court [received] stipulations from the parties and depositions from the parties' experts. The court conducted a 4-day bench trial. It heard, among other testimony, the opinions from expert witnesses for both sides. On the basis of the stipulations, depositions, and testimony, that court [concluded, *inter alia*, that: after the admitting-privileges requirement went into effect, the number of licensed abortion facilities operating in Texas was reduced from more than 40 to just over half as many; if the surgical center provision were to go into effect, the number of abortion facilities would be reduced to as few as seven or eight; these abortion facilities would exist only in the state's major metropolitan areas;] the suggestion that "that these seven or eight providers could meet the demand of the entire state stretches credulity"[; these reductions would greatly increase travel distances for many women in the state;] "[t]he great weight of evidence demonstrates that, before the act's passage, abortion in Texas was extremely safe with particularly low rates of serious complications and virtually no deaths occurring on account of the procedure"[; "a]bortion, as regulated by the State before the enactment of House Bill 2, has been shown to be much safer, in terms of minor and serious complications, than many common medical procedures not subject to such intense regulation and scrutiny"[; and t]he "cost of coming into compliance" with the surgical-center requirement "for existing clinics is significant," "undisputedly approach[ing] 1 million dollars," and "most likely exceed[ing] 1.5 million dollars," with "[s]ome . . . clinics" unable to "comply due to physical size limitations of their sites." [Based on these findings, the district court enjoined both provisions of the Texas law, but that ruling was reversed by a panel of the U.S. Court of Appeals for the Fifth Circuit.] * * *

III.   *Undue Burden—Legal Standard*

[The] Court of Appeals wrote that a state law is "constitutional if: (1) it does not have the purpose or effect of placing a substantial obstacle in the path of a woman seeking an abortion of a nonviable fetus; and (2) it is reasonably related to (or designed to further) a legitimate state interest." The Court of Appeals went on to hold that "the district court erred by substituting its own judgment for that of the legislature" when it conducted its "undue burden inquiry," in part because "medical uncertainty underlying a statute is for resolution by legislatures, not the courts." (citing *Gonzales v. Carhart,* 550 U.S. 124 (2007)).

CoA is
incorrect

The Court of Appeals' articulation of the relevant standard is incorrect. The first part of the Court of Appeals' test may be read to imply that a district court should not consider the existence or nonexistence of medical benefits when considering whether a regulation of abortion constitutes an undue burden. The rule announced in *Casey,* however, requires that courts consider the burdens a law imposes on abortion access together with the benefits those laws confer. And the second part of the test is wrong to equate the judicial review applicable to the regulation of a constitutionally protected personal liberty with the less strict review applicable where, for example, economic legislation is at issue. See *Williamson v. Lee Optical of Okla., Inc.,* [Ch. 5, Sec. 3]. The Court of Appeals' approach simply does not match the standard that this Court laid out in *Casey,* which asks courts to consider whether any burden imposed on abortion access is "undue."

The statement that legislatures, and not courts, must resolve questions of medical uncertainty is also inconsistent with this Court's case law. Instead, the Court, when determining the constitutionality of laws regulating abortion procedures, has placed considerable weight upon evidence and argument presented in judicial proceedings. In *Casey,* for example, we relied heavily on the District Court's factual findings and the research-based submissions of *amici* in declaring a portion of the law at issue unconstitutional. [And], in *Gonzales* the Court, while pointing out that we must review legislative "factfinding under a deferential standard," added that we must not "place dispositive weight" on those "findings." *Gonzales* went on to point out that the "*Court retains an independent constitutional duty to review factual findings where constitutional rights are at stake.*" (Emphasis added). Although there we upheld a statute regulating abortion, we did not do so solely on the basis of legislative findings explicitly set forth in the statute, noting that "evidence presented in the District Courts contradicts" some of the legislative findings. In these circumstances, we said, "[u]ncritical deference to Congress' factual findings . . . is inappropriate."

Unlike in *Gonzales,* the relevant statute here does not set forth any legislative findings. Rather, one is left to infer that the legislature sought to further a constitutionally acceptable objective (namely, protecting women's health). For a district court to give significant weight to evidence in the judicial record in these circumstances is consistent with this Court's case law. [The] District Court [did] not simply substitute its own judgment for that of the legislature. It considered the evidence in the record— including expert evidence, presented in stipulations, depositions, and testimony. It then weighed the asserted benefits against the burdens. We hold that, in so doing, the District Court applied the correct legal standard.

IV. *Undue Burden—Admitting-Privileges Requirement*

[Before] the enactment of H.B. 2, doctors who provided abortions were required to "have admitting privileges *or* have a working arrangement with a physician(s) who has admitting privileges at a local hospital in order to ensure the necessary back up for medical complications." The new law changed this requirement by requiring that a "physician performing or inducing an abortion . . . must, on the date the abortion is performed or induced, have active admitting privileges at a hospital that . . . is located not further than 30 miles from the location at which the abortion is performed or induced." [The] purpose of the admitting-privileges requirement is to help ensure that women have easy access to a hospital should complications arise during an abortion procedure. But the District Court found that it brought about no such health-related benefit. The court found that "[t]he great weight of evidence demonstrates that, before the act's passage, abortion in Texas was extremely safe with particularly low rates of serious complications and virtually no deaths occurring on account of the procedure." Thus, there was no significant health-related problem that the new law helped to cure.

[When] directly asked at oral argument whether Texas knew of a single instance in which the new requirement would have helped even one woman obtain better treatment, Texas admitted that there was no evidence in the record of such a case. This answer is consistent with the findings of the other Federal District Courts that have considered the health benefits of other States' similar admitting-privileges laws.

[An *amicus*] brief describes the undisputed general fact that "hospitals often condition admitting privileges on reaching a certain number of admissions per year." Returning to the District Court record, we note that, in direct testimony, the president of Nova Health Systems, implicitly relying on this general fact, pointed out that it would be difficult for doctors regularly performing abortions at the El Paso clinic to obtain admitting privileges at nearby hospitals because "[d]uring the past 10 years, over 17,000 abortion procedures were performed at the El Paso clinic [and n]ot a single one of those patients had to be transferred to a hospital for emergency treatment, much less admitted to the hospital." In a word, doctors would be unable to maintain admitting privileges or obtain those privileges for the future, because the fact that abortions are so safe meant that providers were unlikely to have any patients to admit.

[The] record contains sufficient evidence that the admitting-privileges requirement led to the closure of half of Texas' clinics, or thereabouts. Those closures meant fewer doctors, longer waiting times, and increased crowding. Record evidence also supports the finding that after the admitting-privileges provision went into effect, the "number of women of reproductive age living in a county . . . more than 150 miles from a provider increased from approximately 86,000 to 400,000 . . . and the number of women living in a county more than 200 miles from a provider from approximately 10,000 to 290,000." We recognize that increased driving distances do not always constitute an "undue burden." See *Casey* (joint opinion). But here, those increases are but one additional burden, which, when taken together with others that the closings brought about, and when viewed in light of the virtual absence of any health benefit, lead us to conclude that the record adequately supports the District Court's "undue burden" conclusion.

The dissent [argues that some] clinics may have closed for other reasons [but] petitioners satisfied their burden to present evidence of causation by presenting direct testimony as well as plausible inferences to be drawn from the timing of the clinic closures. The District Court credited that evidence and concluded from it that H.B. 2 in fact led to the clinic closures. The dissent's speculation that perhaps other evidence, not presented at trial or credited by the District Court, might have shown that some clinics closed for unrelated reasons does not provide sufficient ground to disturb the District Court's factual finding on that issue.

In the same breath, the dissent suggests that one benefit of H.B. 2's requirements would be that they might "force unsafe facilities to shut down." [The] dissent points to the Kermit Gosnell scandal. Gosnell, a physician in Pennsylvania, was convicted of first-degree murder and manslaughter. [According to the grand jury report, he] "staffed his facility with unlicensed and indifferent workers, and then let them practice medicine unsupervised" and had "[d]irty facilities; unsanitary instruments; an absence of functioning monitoring and resuscitation equipment; the use of cheap, but dangerous, drugs; illegal procedures; and inadequate emergency access for when things inevitably went wrong." Gosnell's behavior was terribly wrong. But there is no reason to believe that an extra layer of regulation would have affected that behavior. Determined wrongdoers, already ignoring existing statutes and safety measures, are unlikely to be convinced to adopt safe practices by a new overlay of regulations. Regardless, Gosnell's deplorable crimes could escape detection only because his facility went uninspected for more than 15 years. Pre-existing Texas law already contained numerous detailed regulations covering abortion facilities, including a requirement that facilities be inspected at least annually.

[V.] *Undue Burden—Surgical-Center Requirement*

[Prior] to enactment of the [surgical-center] requirement, Texas law required abortion facilities to meet a host of health and safety requirements. Under those pre-existing laws, facilities were subject to annual reporting and recordkeeping requirements; a quality assurance program; personnel policies and staffing requirements, physical and environmental requirements; infection control standards; disclosure requirements; patient-rights standards; and medical- and clinical-services standards, including anesthesia standards. These requirements are policed by random and announced inspections, at least annually, as well as administrative penalties, injunctions, civil penalties, and criminal penalties for certain violations[.]

[There] is considerable evidence in the record supporting the District Court's findings indicating that the statutory provision requiring all abortion facilities to meet all surgical-center standards does not benefit patients and is not necessary. [The] record makes clear that the surgical-center requirement provides no benefit when complications arise in the context of an abortion produced through medication. That is because, in such a case, complications would almost always arise only after the patient has left the facility. The record also contains evidence indicating that abortions taking place in an abortion facility are safe—indeed, safer than numerous procedures that take place outside hospitals and to which Texas does not apply its surgical-center requirements. The total number of deaths in Texas from abortions was five in the period from 2001 to 2012, or about one every two years (that is to say, one out of about 120,000 to 144,000 abortions). Nationwide, childbirth is 14 times more likely than abortion to result in death, but Texas law allows a midwife to oversee childbirth in the patient's own home. Colonoscopy, a procedure that typically takes place outside a hospital (or surgical center) setting, has a mortality rate 10 times higher than an abortion. [T]he mortality rate for liposuction, another outpatient procedure, is 28 times higher than the mortality rate for abortion[ ]. Medical treatment after an incomplete miscarriage often involves a procedure identical to that involved in a nonmedical abortion, but it often takes place outside a hospital or surgical center. And Texas partly or wholly grandfathers (or waives in whole or in part the surgical-center requirement for) about two-thirds of the facilities to which the surgical-center standards apply. But it neither grandfathers nor provides waivers for any of the facilities that perform abortions. [The] record evidence thus supports the ultimate legal conclusion that the surgical-center requirement is not necessary.

[At] the same time, the record provides adequate evidentiary support for the District Court's conclusion that the surgical-center requirement places a substantial obstacle in the path of women seeking an abortion. [In addition], common sense suggests that, more often than not, a physical facility that satisfies a certain physical demand will not be able to meet five times that demand without expanding or otherwise incurring significant costs. Suppose that we know only that a certain grocery store serves 200 customers per week, that a certain apartment building provides apartments for 200 families, that a certain train station welcomes 200 trains per day. While it is conceivable that the store, the apartment building, or the train station could just as easily provide for 1,000 customers, families, or trains at no significant additional cost, crowding, or delay, most of us would find this possibility highly improbable. The dissent takes issue with this general, intuitive point by arguing that many places operate below capacity and that in any event, facilities could simply hire additional providers. We disagree that, according to common sense, medical facilities, well known for their wait times, operate below capacity as a general matter. And the fact that so many facilities were forced to close by the admitting-privileges requirement means that hiring more physicians would not be quite as simple as the dissent suggests. Courts are free to base their findings on commonsense inferences drawn from the evidence. And that is what the District Court did here.

[More] fundamentally, in the face of no threat to women's health, Texas seeks to force women to travel long distances to get abortions in crammed-to-capacity superfacilities. Patients seeking these services are less likely to get the kind of individualized attention, serious conversation, and emotional support that doctors at less taxed facilities may have offered. Healthcare facilities and medical professionals are not fungible commodities. Surgical centers attempting to accommodate sudden, vastly increased demand, may find that quality of care declines. Another commonsense inference that the District Court made is that these effects would be harmful to, not supportive of, women's health. [We] agree with the District Court that the surgical-center requirement, like the admitting-privileges requirement, provides few, if any, health benefits for women, poses a substantial obstacle to women seeking abortions, and constitutes an "undue burden" on their constitutional right to do so. * * *

JUSTICE GINSBURG, concurring.

[When] a State severely limits access to safe and legal procedures, women in desperate circumstances may resort to unlicensed rogue practitioners, *faute de mieux,* at great risk to their health and safety.

JUSTICE THOMAS, dissenting.

[Whatever] scrutiny the majority applies to Texas' law, it bears little resemblance to the undue-burden test the Court articulated in *Casey* and its successors. Instead, the majority eviscerates important features of that test to return to a regime like the one that *Casey* repudiated. I remain fundamentally opposed to the Court's abortion jurisprudence. Even taking *Casey* as the baseline, however, the majority radically rewrites the undue-burden test in three ways. First, today's decision requires courts to "consider the burdens a law imposes on abortion access together with the benefits those laws confer." Second, today's opinion tells the courts that, when the law's justifications are medically uncertain, they need not defer to the legislature, and must instead assess medical justifications for abortion restrictions by scrutinizing the record themselves. Finally, even if a law imposes no "substantial obstacle" to women's access to abortions, the law now must have more than a "reasonabl[e] relat[ion] to . . . a legitimate state interest." These precepts are nowhere to be found in *Casey* or its successors, and transform the undue-burden test to something much more akin to strict scrutiny.

[The] majority's furtive reconfiguration of the standard of scrutiny applicable to abortion restrictions also points to a deeper problem. The undue-burden standard is just one variant of the Court's tiers-of-scrutiny approach to constitutional adjudication. And the label the Court affixes to its level of scrutiny in assessing whether the government can restrict a given right—be it "rational basis," intermediate, strict, or something else— is increasingly a meaningless formalism. As the Court applies whatever standard it likes to any given case, nothing but empty words separates our constitutional decisions from judicial fiat.

Though the tiers of scrutiny have become a ubiquitous feature of constitutional law, they are of recent vintage. Only in the 1960's did the Court begin in earnest to speak of "strict scrutiny" versus reviewing legislation for mere rationality, and to develop the contours of these tests. See Richard H. Fallon, *Strict Judicial Scrutiny*, 54 UCLA L. Rev. 1267 (2007). In short order, the Court adopted strict scrutiny as the standard for reviewing everything from race-based classifications under the Equal Protection Clause to restrictions on constitutionally protected speech. Then the tiers of scrutiny proliferated into ever more gradations. *Casey*'s undue-burden test added yet another right-specific test on the spectrum between rational-basis and strict-scrutiny review.

[If] our recent cases illustrate anything, it is how easily the Court tinkers with levels of scrutiny to achieve its desired result. This Term, it is easier for a State to survive strict scrutiny despite discriminating on the basis of race in college admissions than it is for the same State to regulate how abortion doctors and clinics operate under the putatively less stringent undue-burden test. Likewise, it is now easier for the government to restrict judicial candidates' campaign speech than for the Government to define marriage—even though the former is subject to strict scrutiny and the latter was supposedly subject to some form of rational-basis review. [These] labels now mean little. [The] Court should abandon the pretense that anything other than policy preferences underlies its balancing of constitutional rights and interests in any given case.

[The] Court has simultaneously transformed judicially created rights like the right to abortion into preferred constitutional rights, while disfavoring many of the rights actually enumerated in the Constitution. But our Constitution renounces the notion that some constitutional rights are more equal than others. A plaintiff either possesses the constitutional right he is asserting, or not—and if not, the judiciary has no business creating ad hoc exceptions so that others can assert rights that seem especially important to vindicate. A law either infringes a constitutional right, or not; there is no room for the judiciary to invent tolerable degrees of encroachment. Unless the Court abides by one set of rules to adjudicate constitutional rights, it will continue reducing constitutional law to policy-driven value judgments until the last shreds of its legitimacy disappear.

Today's decision will prompt some to claim victory, just as it will stiffen opponents' will to object. But the entire Nation has lost something essential. The majority's embrace of a jurisprudence of rights-specific exceptions and balancing tests is "a regrettable concession of defeat—an acknowledgement that we have passed the point where 'law,' properly speaking, has any further application." Antonin Scalia, *The Rule of Law as a Law of Rules*, 56 U. Chi. L. Rev. 1175 (1989). I respectfully dissent.

JUSTICE ALITO, with whom the CHIEF JUSTICE and JUSTICE THOMAS join, dissenting.[1]

[Under] our cases, petitioners must show that the admitting privileges and [ambulatory surgical center ("ASC")] requirements impose an "undue burden" on women seeking abortions. And in order to obtain the sweeping relief they seek—facial invalidation of those provisions—they must show, at a minimum, that these provisions have an unconstitutional impact on at least a "large fraction" of Texas women of reproductive age. Such a situation could result if the clinics able to comply with the new requirements either lacked the requisite overall capacity or were located too far away to serve a "large fraction" of the women in question.

Petitioners did not make that showing. Instead of offering direct evidence, they relied on two crude inferences. First, they pointed to the number of abortion clinics that closed after the enactment of H.B. 2, and asked that it be inferred that all these closures resulted from the two challenged provisions. They made little effort to show why particular clinics closed. Second, they pointed to the number of abortions performed annually at ASCs before H.B. 2 took effect and, because this figure is well below the total number of abortions performed each year in the State, they asked that it be inferred that ASC-compliant clinics could not meet the demands of women in the State. Petitioners failed to provide any evidence of the actual capacity of the facilities that would be available to perform abortions in compliance with the new law—even though they provided this type of evidence in their first case to the District Court at trial and then to this Court in their application for interim injunctive relief.

---

[1]   Most of the dissent argued that the plaintiffs' claims were barred by claim preclusion because they had previously brought an unsuccessful pre-enforcement facial challenge to the admitting privileges requirement. It also argued that facial invalidation was an improper remedy because of the Texas law's broad severability clause. The discussion of claim preclusion and severability have been omitted from both the majority and this dissent.

I do not dispute the fact that H.B. 2 caused the closure of some clinics. Indeed, it seems clear that H.B. 2 was intended to force unsafe facilities to shut down. The law was one of many enacted by States in the wake of the Kermit Gosnell scandal, in which a physician who ran an abortion clinic in Philadelphia was convicted for the first-degree murder of three infants who were born alive and for the manslaughter of a patient. Gosnell had not been actively supervised by state or local authorities or by his peers, and the Philadelphia grand jury that investigated the case recommended that the Commonwealth adopt a law requiring abortion clinics to comply with the same regulations as ASCs. If Pennsylvania had had such a requirement in force, the Gosnell facility may have been shut down before his crimes. And if there were any similarly unsafe facilities in Texas, H.B. 2 was clearly intended to put them out of business.

While there can be no doubt that H.B. 2 caused some clinics to cease operation, the absence of proof regarding the reasons for particular closures is a problem because some clinics have or may have closed for at least four reasons other than the two H.B. 2 requirements at issue here. These are:

1.   *H.B. 2's restriction on medication abortion.* In their first case, petitioners challenged the provision of H.B. 2 that regulates medication abortion, but that part of the statute was upheld by the Fifth Circuit and not relitigated in this case. The record in this case indicates that in the first six months after this restriction took effect, the number of medication abortions dropped by 6,957 (compared to the same period the previous year).

2.   *Withdrawal of Texas family planning funds.* In 2011, Texas passed a law preventing family planning grants to providers that perform abortions and their affiliates. In the first case, petitioners' expert admitted that some clinics closed "as a result of the defunding," and [this] withdrawal appears specifically to have caused multiple clinic closures in West Texas.

3.   *The nationwide decline in abortion demand.* Petitioners' expert testimony relies on a study from the Guttmacher Institute which concludes that "the national abortion rate has resumed its decline, and *no evidence was found that the overall drop in abortion incidence was related to the decrease in providers or to restrictions implemented between 2008 and 2011.*" [Citations and internal quotation marks omitted.] Consistent with that trend, "[t]he number of abortions to residents of Texas declined by 4,956 between 2010 and 2011 and by 3,905 between 2011 and 2012."

4.   *Physician retirement (or other localized factors).* Like everyone else, most physicians eventually retire, and the retirement of a physician who performs abortions can cause the closing of a clinic or a reduction in the number of abortions that a clinic can perform. When this happens, the closure of the clinic or the reduction in capacity cannot be attributed to

H.B. 2 unless it is shown that the retirement was caused by the admitting privileges or surgical center requirements as opposed to age or some other factor.

[Neither] petitioners nor the District Court properly addressed these complexities in assessing causation—and for no good reason. [Because] there was ample reason to believe that some closures were caused by these other factors, the District Court's failure to ascertain the reasons for clinic closures means that, on the record before us, there is no way to tell which closures actually count. Petitioners—who, as plaintiffs, bore the burden of proof—cannot simply point to temporal correlation and call it causation.

Even if the District Court had properly filtered out immaterial closures, its analysis would have been incomplete for a second reason. Petitioners offered scant evidence on the capacity of the clinics that are able to comply with the admitting privileges and ASC requirements, or on those clinics' geographic distribution. Reviewing the evidence in the record, it is far from clear that there has been a material impact on access to abortion. [Applying] what the Court terms "common sense," the Court infers that the ASCs that performed abortions at the time of H.B. 2's enactment lacked the capacity to perform all the abortions sought by women in Texas.

[The] Court's inference has obvious limitations. First, it is not unassailable "common sense" to hold that current utilization equals capacity. [Faced] with increased demand, ASCs could potentially increase the number of abortions performed without prohibitively expensive changes. Among other things, they might hire more physicians who perform abortions, utilize their facilities more intensively or efficiently, or shift the mix of services provided. Second, what matters for present purposes is not the capacity of just those ASCs that performed abortions prior to the enactment of H.B. 2 but the capacity of those that would be available to perform abortions after the statute took effect. And since the enactment of H.B. 2, the number of ASCs performing abortions has increased by 50%—from six in 2012 to nine today.

[The] Court asserts that, after the admitting privileges requirement took effect, clinics "were not able to accommodate increased demand," but petitioners' own evidence suggested that the requirement had *no* effect on capacity. On this point, like the question of the reason for clinic closures, petitioners did not discharge their burden, and the District Court did not engage in the type of analysis that should have been conducted before enjoining an important state law.

[I] do not dismiss the situation of those women who would no longer live within 150 miles of a clinic as a result of H.B. 2. But under current doctrine such localized problems can be addressed by narrow as-applied challenges. * * *

NOTES AND QUESTIONS

1. ***"Partial-birth" abortion.*** *Whole Woman's Health* was not the first Supreme Court case since *Planned Parenthood v. Casey* to strike down an abortion regulation as an undue burden. In *Stenberg v. Carhart*, 530 U.S. 914 (2000), a 5–4 majority, per BREYER, J., struck down a Nebraska law forbidding "partial-birth abortion," which the law defined as "an abortion procedure in which the person performing the abortion partially delivers vaginally a living unborn child before killing the unborn child and completing the delivery." The Court found two constitutional deficiencies. First, the Nebraska law did not contain an exception for circumstances in which the proscribed procedure was medically necessary. Second, the definition of the proscribed procedure was insufficiently clear to inform a doctor when she was violating the law, and thus imposed an undue burden.

However, the Court appeared to retreat from these holdings in *Gonzales v. Carhart*, 550 U.S. 124 (2007). Following a change in personnel, a different 5–4 majority, per KENNEDY, J., upheld a federal partial-birth abortion ban. Although the Court purported to distinguish rather than overrule the decision in the Nebraska case, the tone of the opinion in the federal case was different: "Respect for human life finds an ultimate expression in the bond of love the mother has for her child. The Act recognizes this reality," the Court explained, seemingly validating the legislative decision to ban a method of abortion on the ground that a woman might come to regret her decision if she later realized "that she allowed a doctor to pierce the skull and vacuum the fast-developing brain of her unborn child, a child assuming the human form."

According to Reva B. Siegel, *Dignity and the Politics of Protection: Abortion Restrictions Under Casey/Carhart*, 117 Yale L.J. 1694 (2008), the discussion of women who regret having abortions "reflects the spread of abortion restrictions that are woman-protective, as well as fetal-protective, in form and justification. [*Casey*] bases the abortion right [on] the understanding that government cannot enforce customary or common-law understandings of women's roles. [By contrast, the] new gender paternalism [reflected in the woman-protective rationale for abortion restrictions] is in fact the old gender paternalism: laws (1) based on stereotypes about women's capacity and women's roles that (2) deny women agency (3) for the claimed purpose of protecting women from coercion and/or freeing them to be mothers. Gender paternalism of this kind violates the very forms of dignity that *Casey*—and the equal protection cases—protect."

2. ***Health measures.*** Dissenting in the 2007 *Carhart* case, GINSBURG, J., joined by Stevens, Souter, and Breyer, JJ., pointed to lower court findings casting serious doubt on the factual basis for the federal ban. She also noted that "the congressional record includes letters from numerous individual physicians stating that pregnant women's health would be jeopardized under the Act." The majority nonetheless rejected the argument that the federal law was invalid because it endangered women's health, citing "documented medical disagreement." Why is the Court apparently more deferential to the

health claims advanced in support of the law in *Carhart* than in *Whole Woman's Health?*

P. 507, at end of note 1:

KERRY v. DIN, 135 S.Ct. 2128 (2015) rejected a U.S. citizen's claim that she had a right to a full statement of the reasons why the government refused to grant her noncitizen husband an entry visa. SCALIA, J., announced the judgment of the Court and issued an opinion in which Thomas, J., and Roberts, C.J., joined. In addition to rejecting the procedural claim (discussed infra, Sec. 6), the plurality cast doubt on the fundamental right to marry itself, and indeed, on all implied fundamental rights, which it termed "textually unsupportable."

P. 508, substitute for last two paragraphs of note 2:

The Court vindicated the predictions in *Obergefell v. Hodges,* 135 S.Ct. 2584 (2015), set forth immediately below in this Supplement.

P. 569, after note 4:

Same-Sex Marriage (Again)

OBERGEFELL V. HODGES
___ U.S. ___, 135 S.Ct. 2584, 192 L.Ed.2d 609 (2015).

JUSTICE KENNEDY delivered the opinion of the Court.

The Constitution promises liberty to all within its reach, a liberty that includes certain specific rights that allow persons, within a lawful realm, to define and express their identity. The petitioners in these cases seek to find that liberty by marrying someone of the same sex and having their marriages deemed lawful on the same terms and conditions as marriages between persons of the opposite sex.

I.   [The] petitioners are 14 same-sex couples and two men whose same-sex partners are deceased. The respondents are state officials responsible for enforcing the laws in question. The petitioners claim the respondents violate the Fourteenth Amendment by denying them the right to marry or to have their marriages, lawfully performed in another State, given full recognition.

II.   A. [From] their beginning to their most recent page, the annals of human history reveal the transcendent importance of marriage. The lifelong union of a man and a woman always has promised nobility and dignity to all persons, without regard to their station in life. Marriage is sacred to those who live by their religions and offers unique fulfillment to those who find meaning in the secular realm. Its dynamic allows two people to find a life that could not be found alone, for a marriage becomes greater than just the two persons. Rising from the most basic human needs, marriage is essential to our most profound hopes and aspirations.

[The] respondents say [it] would demean a timeless institution if the concept and lawful status of marriage were extended to two persons of the same sex. [Yet f]ar from seeking to devalue marriage, the petitioners seek it for themselves because of their respect—and need—for its privileges and responsibilities. And their immutable nature dictates that same-sex marriage is their only real path to this profound commitment.

B. [Marriage]—even as confined to opposite-sex relations—has evolved over time. For example, marriage was once viewed as an arrangement by the couple's parents based on political, religious, and financial concerns; but by the time of the Nation's founding it was understood to be a voluntary contract between a man and a woman. As the role and status of women changed, the institution further evolved. Under the centuries-old doctrine of coverture, a married man and woman were treated by the State as a single, male-dominated legal entity. See 1 W. Blackstone, Commentaries on the Laws of England 430 (1765). As women gained legal, political, and property rights, and as society began to understand that women have their own equal dignity, the law of coverture was abandoned. These and other developments in the institution of marriage over the past centuries were not mere superficial changes. Rather, they worked deep transformations in its structure, affecting aspects of marriage long viewed by many as essential.

[This] Court first gave detailed consideration to the legal status of homosexuals in *Bowers v. Hardwick*. There it upheld the constitutionality of a Georgia law deemed to criminalize certain homosexual acts. Ten years later, in *Romer v. Evans* (1996) [Ch. 9, Sec. 4, I], the Court invalidated an amendment to Colorado's Constitution that sought to foreclose any branch or political subdivision of the State from protecting persons against discrimination based on sexual orientation. Then, in 2003, the Court overruled *Bowers,* holding that laws making same-sex intimacy a crime "demea[n] the lives of homosexual persons." *Lawrence.* Two Terms ago, in *Windsor* [Ch. 9, Sec. 4, I] this Court invalidated [the Defense of Marriage Act] to the extent it barred the Federal Government from treating same-sex marriages as valid even when they were lawful in the State where they were licensed. DOMA, the Court held, impermissibly disparaged those same-sex couples "who wanted to affirm their commitment to one another before their children, their family, their friends, and their community."

III. [The] right to marry is fundamental under the Due Process Clause. [It] cannot be denied that this Court's cases describing the right to marry presumed a relationship involving opposite-sex partners. The Court, like many institutions, has made assumptions defined by the world and time of which it is a part. Still, [i]n defining the right to marry [our] cases have identified essential attributes of that right based in history, tradition, and other constitutional liberties inherent in this intimate bond. And in assessing whether the force and rationale of its cases apply to same-sex couples, the Court must respect the basic reasons why the right to marry has been long protected. This analysis compels the conclusion that same-sex couples may exercise the right to marry. The four principles and traditions to be discussed demonstrate that the reasons marriage is fundamental under the Constitution apply with equal force to same-sex couples.

A first premise of the Court's relevant precedents is that the right to personal choice regarding marriage is inherent in the concept of individual autonomy. This abiding connection between marriage and liberty is why *Loving* invalidated interracial marriage bans under the Due Process Clause. [The] nature of marriage is that, through its enduring bond, two persons together can find other freedoms, such as expression, intimacy, and spirituality. This is true for all persons, whatever their sexual orientation.

[A] second principle in this Court's jurisprudence is that the right to marry is fundamental because it supports a two-person union unlike any other in its importance to the committed individuals. [Marriage] responds to the universal fear that a lonely person might call out only to find no one there. It offers the hope of companionship and understanding and assurance that while both still live there will be someone to care for the other. As this Court held in *Lawrence,* same-sex couples have the same right as opposite-sex couples to enjoy intimate association. [But] while *Lawrence* confirmed a dimension of freedom that allows individuals to engage in intimate association without criminal liability, it does not follow that freedom stops there. Outlaw to outcast may be a step forward, but it does not achieve the full promise of liberty.

A third basis for protecting the right to marry is that it safeguards children and families and thus draws meaning from related rights of childrearing, procreation, and education. See *Pierce*; *Meyer*. [Under] the laws of the several States, some of marriage's protections for children and families are material. But marriage also confers more profound benefits. By giving recognition and legal structure to their parents' relationship, marriage allows children "to understand the integrity and closeness of their own family and its concord with other families in their community and in their daily lives." *Windsor*. Marriage also affords the permanency and stability important to children's best interests. As all parties agree, many same-sex couples provide loving and nurturing homes to their children, whether biological or adopted. And hundreds of thousands of children are presently being raised by such couples. Most States have allowed gays and lesbians to adopt, either as individuals or as couples, and many adopted and foster children have same-sex parents. This provides powerful confirmation from the law itself that gays and lesbians can create loving, supportive families. [The] marriage laws at issue here thus harm and humiliate the children of same-sex couples.

That is not to say the right to marry is less meaningful for those who do not or cannot have children. An ability, desire, or promise to procreate is not and has not been a prerequisite for a valid marriage in any State. In light of precedent protecting the right of a married couple not to procreate, it cannot be said the Court or the States have conditioned the right to marry on the capacity or commitment to procreate. The constitutional marriage right has many aspects, of which childbearing is only one.

Fourth and finally, this Court's cases and the Nation's traditions make clear that marriage is a keystone of our social order. [While] the States are in general free to vary the benefits they confer on all married couples, they have throughout our history made marriage the basis for an expanding list of governmental rights, benefits, and responsibilities, [including]: taxation; inheritance and property rights; rules of intestate succession; spousal privilege in the law of evidence; hospital access; medical decisionmaking authority; adoption rights; the rights and benefits of survivors; birth and death certificates; professional ethics rules; campaign finance restrictions; workers' compensation benefits; health insurance; and child custody, support, and visitation rules. [The] States have contributed to the fundamental character of the marriage right by placing that institution at the center of so many facets of the legal and social order.

There is no difference between same- and opposite-sex couples with respect to this principle. Yet by virtue of their exclusion from that institution, same-sex couples are denied the constellation of benefits that the States have linked to marriage. This harm results in more than just material burdens. Same-sex couples are consigned to an instability many opposite-sex couples would deem intolerable in their own lives. As the State itself makes marriage all the more precious by the significance it attaches to it, exclusion from that status has the effect of teaching that gays and lesbians are unequal in important respects. It demeans gays and lesbians for the State to lock them out of a central institution of the Nation's society. [Laws] excluding same-sex couples from the marriage right impose stigma and injury of the kind prohibited by our basic charter.

[Respondents invoke] *Glucksberg*, which called for a " 'careful description' " of fundamental rights. [*Glucksberg*] did insist that liberty under the Due Process Clause must be defined in a most circumscribed manner, with central reference to specific historical practices. Yet while that approach may have been appropriate for the asserted right there involved (physician-assisted suicide), it is inconsistent with the approach this Court has used in discussing other fundamental rights, including marriage and intimacy. *Loving* did not ask about a "right to interracial marriage"; *Turner* did not ask about a "right of inmates to marry"; and

Zablocki did not ask about a "right of fathers with unpaid child support duties to marry." [If] rights were defined by who exercised them in the past, then received practices could serve as their own continued justification and new groups could not invoke rights once denied.

[Many] who deem same-sex marriage to be wrong reach that conclusion based on decent and honorable religious or philosophical premises, and neither they nor their beliefs are disparaged here. But when that sincere, personal opposition becomes enacted law and public policy, the necessary consequence is to put the imprimatur of the State itself on an exclusion that soon demeans or stigmatizes those whose own liberty is then denied.

[The] right of same-sex couples to marry that is part of the liberty promised by the Fourteenth Amendment is derived, too, from that Amendment's guarantee of the equal protection of the laws. The Due Process Clause and the Equal Protection Clause are connected in a profound way, though they set forth independent principles. Rights implicit in liberty and rights secured by equal protection may rest on different precepts and are not always co-extensive, yet in some instances each may be instructive as to the meaning and reach of the other. In any particular case one Clause may be thought to capture the essence of the right in a more accurate and comprehensive way, even as the two Clauses may converge in the identification and definition of the right. This interrelation of the two principles furthers our understanding of what freedom is and must become.

[In] interpreting the Equal Protection Clause, the Court has recognized that new insights and societal understandings can reveal unjustified inequality within our most fundamental institutions that once passed unnoticed and unchallenged. To take but one period, this occurred with respect to marriage in the 1970's and 1980's. Notwithstanding the gradual erosion of the doctrine of coverture, invidious sex-based classifications in marriage remained common through the mid-20th century. These classifications denied the equal dignity of men and women. One State's law, for example, provided in 1971 that "the husband is the head of the family and the wife is subject to him; her legal civil existence is merged in the husband, except so far as the law recognizes her separately, either for her own protection, or for her benefit." Ga.Code Ann. § 53–501 (1935). Responding to a new awareness, the Court invoked equal protection principles to invalidate laws imposing sex-based inequality on marriage. [Numerous citations omitted.] Like *Loving* and *Zablocki,* these precedents show the Equal Protection Clause can help to identify and correct inequalities in the institution of marriage, vindicating precepts of liberty and equality under the Constitution.

[This] dynamic also applies to same-sex marriage. [T]he marriage laws enforced by the respondents are in essence unequal: same-sex couples are denied all the benefits afforded to opposite-sex couples and are barred from exercising a fundamental right. Especially against a long history of disapproval of their relationships, this denial to same-sex couples of the right to marry works a grave and continuing harm.

[The] Court now holds that same-sex couples may exercise the fundamental right to marry. No longer may this liberty be denied to them. [T]he State laws challenged by Petitioners in these cases are now held invalid to the extent they exclude same-sex couples from civil marriage on the same terms and conditions as opposite-sex couples.

IV. [The] respondents warn there has been insufficient democratic discourse before deciding an issue so basic as the definition of marriage. [Yet] there has been far more deliberation than this argument acknowledges. There have been referenda, legislative debates, and grassroots campaigns, as well as countless studies, papers, books, and other popular and scholarly writings. There has been extensive litigation in state and federal courts. [An Appendix listed lower court cases.] Judicial opinions addressing the issue have been informed by the contentions of parties and counsel, which, in turn, reflect the more general, societal discussion of same-sex marriage and its meaning that has occurred over the past decades. [Many] of the central institutions in American life—state and local governments, the military, large and small businesses, labor unions, religious organizations, law enforcement, civic groups, professional organizations, and universities—have devoted substantial attention to the question. This has led to an enhanced understanding of the issue—an understanding reflected in the arguments now presented for resolution as a matter of constitutional law.

The dynamic of our constitutional system is that individuals need not await legislative action before asserting a fundamental right. The Nation's courts are open to injured individuals who come to them to vindicate their own direct, personal stake in our basic charter. [It] is of no moment whether advocates of same-sex marriage now enjoy or lack momentum in the democratic process.

[The] respondents also argue allowing same-sex couples to wed will harm marriage as an institution by leading to fewer opposite-sex marriages. This may occur, the respondents contend, because licensing same-sex marriage severs the connection between natural procreation and marriage. That argument, however, rests on a counterintuitive view of opposite-sex couple's decisionmaking processes regarding marriage and parenthood. Decisions about whether to marry and raise children are based on many personal, romantic, and practical considerations; and it is unrealistic to conclude that an opposite-sex couple would choose not to marry simply because same-sex couples may do so.

[Finally], it must be emphasized that religions, and those who adhere to religious doctrines, may continue to advocate with utmost, sincere conviction that, by divine precepts, same-sex marriage should not be condoned. The First Amendment ensures that religious organizations and persons are given proper protection as they seek to teach the principles that are so fulfilling and so central to their lives and faiths, and to their own deep aspirations to continue the family structure they have long revered. The same is true of those who oppose same-sex marriage for other reasons. In turn, those who believe allowing same-sex marriage is proper or indeed essential, whether as a matter of religious conviction or secular belief, may engage those who disagree with their view in an open and searching debate. The Constitution, however, does not permit the State to bar same-sex couples from marriage on the same terms as accorded to couples of the opposite sex.

V.   These cases also present the question whether the Constitution requires States to recognize same-sex marriages validly performed out of State. [The] Court, in this decision, holds same-sex couples may exercise the fundamental right to marry in all States. It follows that the Court also must hold—and it now does hold—that there is no lawful basis for a State to refuse to recognize a lawful same-sex marriage performed in another State on the ground of its same-sex character.

* * *

No union is more profound than marriage, for it embodies the highest ideals of love, fidelity, devotion, sacrifice, and family. In forming a marital union, two people become something greater than once they were. As some of the petitioners in these cases demonstrate, marriage embodies a love that may endure even past death. It would misunderstand these men and women to say they disrespect the idea of marriage. Their plea is that they do respect it, respect it so deeply that they seek to find its fulfillment for themselves. Their hope is not to be condemned to live in loneliness, excluded from one of civilization's oldest institutions. They ask for equal dignity in the eyes of the law. The Constitution grants them that right.

CHIEF JUSTICE ROBERTS, with whom JUSTICE SCALIA and JUSTICE THOMAS join, dissenting.

[Although] the policy arguments for extending marriage to same-sex couples may be compelling, the legal arguments for requiring such an extension are not. The fundamental right to marry does not include a right to make a State change its definition of marriage. And a State's decision to maintain the meaning of marriage that has persisted in every culture throughout human history can hardly be called irrational. In short, our Constitution does not enact any one theory of marriage. The people of a

State are free to expand marriage to include same-sex couples, or to retain the historic definition.

Today, however, the Court takes the extraordinary step of ordering every State to license and recognize same-sex marriage. Many people will rejoice at this decision, and I begrudge none their celebration. But for those who believe in a government of laws, not of men, the majority's approach is deeply disheartening. Supporters of same-sex marriage have achieved considerable success persuading their fellow citizens—through the democratic process—to adopt their view. That ends today. Five lawyers have closed the debate and enacted their own vision of marriage as a matter of constitutional law. Stealing this issue from the people will for many cast a cloud over same-sex marriage, making a dramatic social change that much more difficult to accept.

[The] Court invalidates the marriage laws of more than half the States and orders the transformation of a social institution that has formed the basis of human society for millennia, for the Kalahari Bushmen and the Han Chinese, the Carthaginians and the Aztecs. Just who do we think we are?

It can be tempting for judges to confuse our own preferences with the requirements of the law. But as this Court has been reminded throughout our history, the Constitution "is made for people of fundamentally differing views." *Lochner* (Holmes, J., dissenting). [The majority] seizes for itself a question the Constitution leaves to the people, at a time when the people are engaged in a vibrant debate on that question.

I.   [Petitioners] and their *amici* base their arguments on the "right to marry" and the imperative of "marriage equality." There is no serious dispute that, under our precedents, the Constitution protects a right to marry and requires States to apply their marriage laws equally. The real question in these cases is what constitutes "marriage," or—more precisely—*who decides* what constitutes "marriage"? The majority largely ignores these questions, relegating ages of human experience with marriage to a paragraph or two.

A.   [The] universal definition of marriage as the union of a man and a woman is no historical coincidence. Marriage did not come about as a result of a political movement, discovery, disease, war, religious doctrine, or any other moving force of world history—and certainly not as a result of a prehistoric decision to exclude gays and lesbians. It arose in the nature of things to meet a vital need: ensuring that children are conceived by a mother and father committed to raising them in the stable conditions of a lifelong relationship.

The premises supporting this concept of marriage are so fundamental that they rarely require articulation. The human race must procreate to survive. Procreation occurs through sexual relations between a man and a woman. When sexual relations result in the conception of a child, that child's prospects are generally better if the mother and father stay together rather than going their separate ways. Therefore, for the good of children and society, sexual relations that can lead to procreation should occur only between a man and a woman committed to a lasting bond. Society has recognized that bond as marriage. And by bestowing a respected status and material benefits on married couples, society encourages men and women to conduct sexual relations within marriage rather than without.

[This] singular understanding of marriage has prevailed in the United States throughout our history. [Early] Americans drew heavily on legal scholars like William Blackstone, who regarded marriage between "husband and wife" as one of the "great relations in private life," and philosophers like John Locke, who described marriage as "a voluntary compact between man and woman" centered on "its chief end, procreation" and the "nourishment and support" of children.

[As] the majority notes, some aspects of marriage have changed over time. Arranged marriages have largely given way to pairings based on romantic love. States have replaced coverture, the doctrine by which a married man and woman became a single legal entity, with laws that respect each participant's separate status. Racial restrictions on marriage, which "arose as an incident to slavery" to promote "White Supremacy," were repealed by many States and ultimately struck down by this Court. *Loving.* [But] these developments [did not] work any transformation in the core structure of marriage as the union between a man and a woman. If you had asked a person on the street how marriage was defined, no one would ever have said, "Marriage is the union of a man and a woman, where the woman is subject to coverture." The majority may be right that the "history of marriage is one of both continuity and change," but the core meaning of marriage has endured.

II.   [The] majority purports to identify four "principles and traditions" in this Court's due process precedents that support a fundamental right for same-sex couples to marry. *Ante,* at 12. In reality, however, the majority's approach has no basis in principle or tradition, except for the unprincipled tradition of judicial policymaking that characterized discredited decisions such as *Lochner.*

A.   [To] avoid repeating *Lochner*'s error of converting personal preferences into constitutional mandates, our modern substantive due process cases have stressed the need for "judicial self-restraint." *Collins v. Harker Heights,* 503 U.S. 115 (1992). Our precedents have required that implied fundamental rights be "objectively, deeply rooted in this Nation's history and tradition," and "implicit in the concept of ordered liberty, such that neither liberty nor justice would exist if they were sacrificed." *Glucksberg.* Although the Court articulated the importance of history and tradition to the fundamental rights inquiry most precisely in *Glucksberg*, many other cases both before and after have adopted the same approach.

Proper reliance on history and tradition of course requires looking beyond the individual law being challenged, so that every restriction on liberty does not supply its own constitutional justification. The Court is right about that. But given the few "guideposts for responsible decisionmaking in this unchartered area," *Collins*, "an approach grounded in history imposes limits on the judiciary that are more meaningful than any based on [an] abstract formula." *Moore*.

B.   The majority acknowledges none of this doctrinal background, and it is easy to see why: Its aggressive application of substantive due process breaks sharply with decades of precedent and returns the Court to the unprincipled approach of *Lochner*.

1.   [Prior] cases do not hold, of course, that anyone who wants to get married has a constitutional right to do so. They instead require a State to justify barriers to marriage as that institution has always been understood. In *Loving*, the Court held that racial restrictions on the right to marry lacked a compelling justification. In *Zablocki*, restrictions based on child support debts did not suffice. In *Turner*, restrictions based on status as a prisoner were deemed impermissible.

None of the laws at issue in those cases purported to change the core definition of marriage as the union of a man and a woman. The laws challenged in *Zablocki* and *Turner* did not define marriage as "the union of a man and a woman, *where neither party owes child support or is in prison.*" Nor did the interracial marriage ban at issue in *Loving* define marriage as "the union of a man and a woman *of the same race.*" Removing racial barriers to marriage therefore did not change what a marriage was any more than integrating schools changed what a school was. As the majority admits, the institution of "marriage" discussed in every one of these cases "presumed a relationship involving opposite-sex partners." In short, the "right to marry" cases stand for the important but limited proposition that particular restrictions on access to marriage *as traditionally defined* violate due process. These precedents say nothing at all about a right to make a State change its definition of marriage, which is the right petitioners actually seek here.

2.   [Neither] *Lawrence* nor any other precedent in the privacy line of cases supports the right that petitioners assert here. Unlike criminal laws banning contraceptives and sodomy, the marriage laws at issue here involve no government intrusion. They create no crime and impose no punishment. Same-sex couples remain free to live together, to engage in intimate conduct, and to raise their families as they see fit. No one is "condemned to live in loneliness" by the laws challenged in these cases—no one. At the same time, [the] privacy cases provide no support for the

majority's position, because petitioners do not seek privacy. Quite the opposite, they seek public recognition of their relationships, along with corresponding government benefits.

3.   [One] immediate question invited by the majority's position is whether States may retain the definition of marriage as a union of two people. Although the majority randomly inserts the adjective "two" in various places, it offers no reason at all why the two-person element of the core definition of marriage may be preserved while the man-woman element may not. Indeed, from the standpoint of history and tradition, a leap from opposite-sex marriage to same-sex marriage is much greater than one from a two-person union to plural unions, which have deep roots in some cultures around the world. [I] do not mean to equate marriage between same-sex couples with plural marriages in all respects. There may well be relevant differences that compel different legal analysis. But if there are, petitioners have not pointed to any.

III. In addition to their due process argument, petitioners contend that the Equal Protection Clause requires their States to license and recognize same-sex marriages. [Yet] the majority fails to provide even a single sentence explaining how the Equal Protection Clause supplies independent weight for its position. [In] any event, the marriage laws at issue here do not violate the Equal Protection Clause, because distinguishing between opposite-sex and same-sex couples is rationally related to the States' "legitimate state interest" in "preserving the traditional institution of marriage." *Lawrence* (O'Connor, J., concurring in judgment).

[The] equal protection analysis might be different, in my view, if we were confronted with a more focused challenge to the denial of certain tangible benefits. Of course, those more selective claims will not arise now that the Court has taken the drastic step of requiring every State to license and recognize marriages between same-sex couples.

IV. Nowhere is the majority's extravagant conception of judicial supremacy more evident than in its description—and dismissal—of the public debate regarding same-sex marriage. Yes, the majority concedes, on one side are thousands of years of human history in every society known to have populated the planet. But on the other side, there has been "extensive litigation," "many thoughtful District Court decisions," "countless studies, papers, books, and other popular and scholarly writings," and "more than 100" *amicus* briefs in these cases alone. What would be the point of allowing the democratic process to go on? It is high time for the Court to decide the meaning of marriage, based on five lawyers' "better informed understanding" of "a liberty that remains urgent in our own era." The answer is surely there in one of those *amicus* briefs or studies.

[By] deciding this question under the Constitution, the Court removes it from the realm of democratic decision. There will be consequences to shutting down the political process on an issue of such profound public significance. Closing debate tends to close minds. People denied a voice are less likely to accept the ruling of a court on an issue that does not seem to be the sort of thing courts usually decide. [H]owever heartened the proponents of same-sex marriage might be on this day, it is worth acknowledging what they have lost, and lost forever: the opportunity to win the true acceptance that comes from persuading their fellow citizens of the justice of their cause. And they lose this just when the winds of change were freshening at their backs.

[Respect] for sincere religious conviction has led voters and legislators in every State that has adopted same-sex marriage democratically to include accommodations for religious practice. The majority's decision imposing same-sex marriage cannot, of course, create any such accommodations. The majority graciously suggests that religious believers may continue to "advocate" and "teach" their views of marriage. The First Amendment guarantees, however, the freedom to *"exercise"* religion. Ominously, that is not a word the majority uses.

* * *

[If] you are among the many Americans—of whatever sexual orientation—who favor expanding same-sex marriage, by all means celebrate today's decision. Celebrate the achievement of a desired goal. Celebrate the opportunity for a new expression of commitment to a partner. Celebrate the availability of new benefits. But do not celebrate the Constitution. It had nothing to do with it.

JUSTICE SCALIA, with whom JUSTICE THOMAS joins, dissenting.

[When] the Fourteenth Amendment was ratified in 1868, every State limited marriage to one man and one woman, and no one doubted the constitutionality of doing so. That resolves these cases. When it comes to determining the meaning of a vague constitutional provision—such as "due process of law" or "equal protection of the laws"—it is unquestionable that the People who ratified that provision did not understand it to prohibit a practice that remained both universal and uncontroversial in the years after ratification. We have no basis for striking down a practice that is not expressly prohibited by the Fourteenth Amendment's text, and that bears the endorsement of a long tradition of open, widespread, and unchallenged use dating back to the Amendment's ratification. Since there is no doubt whatever that the People never decided to prohibit the limitation of marriage to opposite-sex couples, the public debate over same-sex marriage must be allowed to continue.

[Hubris] is sometimes defined as o'erweening pride; and pride, we know, goeth before a fall. The Judiciary is the "least dangerous" of the federal branches because it has "neither Force nor Will, but merely judgment; and must ultimately depend upon the aid of the executive arm" and the States, "even for the efficacy of its judgments."[26] With each decision of ours that takes from the People a question properly left to them—with each decision that is unabashedly based not on law, but on the "reasoned judgment" of a bare majority of this Court—we move one step closer to being reminded of our impotence.

JUSTICE THOMAS, with whom JUSTICE SCALIA joins, dissenting.

[In] the American legal tradition, liberty has long been understood as individual freedom *from* governmental action, not as a right *to* a particular governmental entitlement. [The] founding-era idea of civil liberty as natural liberty constrained by human law necessarily involved only those freedoms that existed *outside of* government.

[Petitioners] cannot claim [that] the States have restricted their ability to go about their daily lives as they would be able to absent governmental restrictions. Petitioners do not ask this Court to order the States to stop restricting their ability to enter same-sex relationships, to engage in intimate behavior, to make vows to their partners in public ceremonies, to engage in religious wedding ceremonies, to hold themselves out as married, or to raise children. The States have imposed no such restrictions. Nor have the States prevented petitioners from approximating a number of incidents of marriage through private legal means, such as wills, trusts, and powers of attorney.

Instead, the States have refused to grant them governmental entitlements. Petitioners claim that as a matter of "liberty," they are entitled to access privileges and benefits that exist solely *because of* the government. [But] receiving governmental recognition and benefits has nothing to do with any understanding of "liberty" that the Framers would have recognized.

JUSTICE ALITO, with whom JUSTICE SCALIA and JUSTICE THOMAS join, dissenting.

[Today], more than 40% of all children in this country are born to unmarried women. This development undoubtedly is both a cause and a result of changes in our society's understanding of marriage. While, for many, the attributes of marriage in 21st-century America have changed, those States that do not want to recognize same-sex marriage have not yet given up on the traditional understanding. They worry that by officially abandoning the older understanding, they may contribute to marriage's further decay. It is far beyond the outer reaches of this Court's authority to say that a State may not adhere to the understanding of marriage that has long prevailed, not just in this country and others with similar cultural

---

[26]   [Ct's Note] *The Federalist* No. 78 (A. Hamilton).

roots, but also in a great variety of countries and cultures all around the globe.

[Today's] decision [will] be used to vilify Americans who are unwilling to assent to the new orthodoxy. In the course of its opinion, the majority compares traditional marriage laws to laws that denied equal treatment for African-Americans and women. The implications of this analogy will be exploited by those who are determined to stamp out every vestige of dissent. Perhaps recognizing how its reasoning may be used, the majority attempts, toward the end of its opinion, to reassure those who oppose same-sex marriage that their rights of conscience will be protected. We will soon see whether this proves to be true. I assume that those who cling to old beliefs will be able to whisper their thoughts in the recesses of their homes, but if they repeat those views in public, they will risk being labeled as bigots and treated as such by governments, employers, and schools.

NOTES AND QUESTIONS

1.   *Synergy.* What does the majority mean when it says that there is a "synergy" between substantive due process and equal protection? Consider Michael C. Dorf, *In Defense of Justice Kennedy's Soaring Language*, www. scotusblog.com/2015/06/symposium-in-defense-of-justice-kennedys-soaring-language (June 27, 2015, last visited May 29, 2016): "equal protection considerations help explain why a right to same-sex marriage does not necessarily open the door to polygamy, adult incest, and the other supposed horribles in the [dissenters'] gay shame parade. With a few notable exceptions, for thousands of years people have been stigmatized, beaten, and killed for the sin of loving someone of the same sex. The dissenters regard this shameful history only as the basis for continued denial of constitutional rights. The majority, by contrast, sees in this history of subordination a special reason to be skeptical of the reasons advanced for excluding same-sex couples from the institution of marriage."

2.   *Polygamy.* Are there practical reasons for concluding that the grounds supporting a right to same-sex marriage need not entail polygamy? Consider Richard A. Posner, *The Chief Justice's Dissent is Heartless*, www. slate.com/articles/news_and_politics/the_breakfast_table/features/2015/scotus _roundup/supreme_court_gay_marriage_john_roberts_dissent_in_obergefell_ is_heartless.html (June 27, 2015, last visited May 29, 2016): "On the first page of [the Chief Justice's dissent], we read that 'marriage has existed for millennia and across civilizations,' and 'for all those millennia, across all those civilizations, marriage referred to only one relationship: the union of a man and a woman.' That's nonsense; polygamy—the union of one man with more than one woman (sometimes with hundreds of women)—has long been common in many civilizations (let's not forget Utah) and remains so in much of the vast Muslim world. But later in his opinion the chief justice remembers polygamy and suggests that if gay marriage is allowed, so must be polygamy. He ignores the fact that polygamy imposes real costs, by reducing the number of

marriageable women. Suppose a society contains 100 men and 100 women, but the five wealthiest men have a total of 50 wives. That leaves 95 men to compete for only 50 marriageable women." Even if Judge Posner is wrong and Chief Justice Roberts is right about whether polygamy can be readily distinguished, should that count as a reason to deny same-sex couples the right to marry?

3. ***The conservatism of the Court's ruling.*** For many years, some LGBTQ activists worried that seeking a legal right to same-sex marriage would distract attention from more pressing concerns and reinforce the norm of marriage as against alternative relationships. With its focus on the dignity of marriage, the ruling in *Obergefell* did not allay those fears. Consider Katherine Franke, *A Progressive Agenda for Married Queers*, http://www.slate.com/blogs/outward/2015/06/30/same_sex_marriage_and_progressive_politics_can_they_coexist.html (June 30, 2015, last visited June 15, 2017): "Since the Supreme Court constitutionalized a right to marriage for same-sex couples, [most] social critics have cautioned that there remain many more items on the gay rights to-do list: enacting antidiscrimination laws, addressing transphobia and the high incidence of homelessness among LGBTQ teens, allaying the disproportionate number of LGBTQ people in immigrant detention, ending homophobic bullying and violence in the schools, and remedying the over-criminalization of people of color in the LGBTQ community. The list, as you can see, is long. But as we redirect our energies and resources to those causes, it's also important to recognize that marriage itself remains a space worthy of ongoing critical attention. Once the gay pride dust has settled, we should expect to see 'nose-holding' pragmatists marry to protect their legal and economic interests even as they remain ambivalent about the institution."

4. THE RIGHT TO KEEP AND BEAR ARMS

P. 595, at end of note 5:

In CAETANO v. MASSACHUSETTS, 136 S.Ct. 1027 (2016), the Court summarily reversed a decision of the Massachusetts Supreme Judicial Court. That Court had found that "stun guns" are not protected arms within the meaning of the Second Amendment because, *inter alia*, "they were not in common use at the time of the Second Amendment's enactment." In a brief *per curiam* opinion, the U.S. Supreme Court explained that this mode of analysis was inconsistent with *Heller*, which makes the relevant question whether a type of arms is in common use today. The Court did not reach the question whether, under the correct test, stun guns are protected arms. ALITO, J., joined by Thomas, J., concurred, but would have gone further to hold that stun guns fall within the Second Amendment's protection. The concurrence argued that it would be perverse to protect self-defense by lethal means but not by non-lethal means.

5. THE DEATH PENALTY AND RELATED PROBLEMS: CRUEL AND UNUSUAL PUNISHMENT

IV. ADDITIONAL CONSTITUTIONAL LIMITS ON IMPOSING SEVERE PUNISHMENT

P. 616, at end of fn. 376:

In *Moore v. Texas*, 137 S.Ct. 1039 (2017), the Court, per GINSBURG, J., held that *Hall* precluded a state court from relying on "superseded medical standards" to conclude that the petitioner was not intellectually disabled for purposes of *Atkins*. ROBERTS, C.J., joined by Thomas and Alito, JJ., dissented on the ground that the petitioner failed to present adequate evidence of intellectual disability, but agreed with the majority that the state's use of outdated factors was impermissible.

P. 620, at end of Sec. 5:

In GLOSSIP v. GROSS, 135 S.Ct. 2726 (2015), the Court confronted a state effort to circumvent the shortage of familiar execution drugs by administering midazolam, an anti-anxiety medication, as the first step of a three-drug protocol. Petitioners argued that midazolam posed an unconstitutional risk that they would not be fully sedated throughout the administration of the remaining drugs, and thus would suffer excruciating pain. The Court, per ALITO, J., disagreed, concluding that "petitioners have not proved that any risk posed by midazolam is substantial when compared to known and available alternative methods of execution. Second, they have failed to establish that the District Court committed clear error when it found that the use of midazolam will not result in severe pain and suffering" in violation of the constitutional standard set forth in *Baze*. Notably, the Court did not accept the petitioners' contention that midazolam's risks ought to be evaluated relative to those of sodium thiopental and pentobarbital, as those drugs had been rendered unavailable due to the lobbying efforts of anti-death penalty activists.

SOTOMAYOR, J., joined by Ginsburg, Breyer, and Kagan, JJ., dissented. She cited a botched Oklahoma execution using midazolam. Although acknowledging that the new state protocol quintupled the dosage, she cited evidence that midazolam is subject to a "ceiling effect" in which increasing the dosage does not increase its effect.

BREYER, J., joined by Ginsburg, J., also dissented. He urged that the Court reconsider its conclusion that the post-*Furman* death penalty statutes satisfy the Eighth Amendment: "In 1976, the Court thought that the constitutional infirmities in the death penalty could be healed; the Court in effect delegated significant responsibility to the States to develop procedures that would protect against those constitutional problems. Almost 40 years of studies, surveys, and experience strongly indicate, however, that this effort has failed. Today's administration of the death penalty involves three fundamental constitutional defects: (1) serious unreliability, (2) arbitrariness in application, and (3) unconscionably long delays that undermine the death penalty's penological purpose. Perhaps as a result, (4) most places within the United States have abandoned its use."

SCALIA, J., joined by Thomas, J., concurred: "If we were to travel down the path that Justice Breyer sets out for us and once again consider the constitutionality of the death penalty, I would ask that counsel also brief whether our cases that have abandoned the historical understanding of the Eighth Amendment, beginning with *Trop*, should be overruled. That case has caused more mischief to our jurisprudence, to our federal system, and to our society than any other that comes to mind. Justice Breyer's dissent is the living refutation of *Trop*'s assumption that this Court has the capacity to recognize "evolving standards of decency." Time and again, the People have voted to exact the death penalty as punishment for the most serious of crimes. Time and again, this Court has upheld that decision. And time and again, a vocal minority of this Court has insisted that things have 'changed radically,' and has sought to replace the judgments of the People with their own standards of decency."

THOMAS, J., joined by Scalia, J., also concurred, emphasizing the egregiousness of the crimes committed by litigants whose claims had either been rejected or accepted by the Court.

6. PROCEDURAL DUE PROCESS IN NON-CRIMINAL CASES

I. DEPRIVATION OF "LIBERTY" AND "PROPERTY" INTERESTS

P. 629, at end of note 8:

In KERRY v. DIN, 135 S.Ct. 2128 (2015), the Court rejected a procedural due process complaint from a citizen whose noncitizen husband was denied a visa to enter the country, apparently on the ground that his work as a payroll clerk in Afghanistan during the period of Taliban rule counted as support for terrorism in violation of a federal statute governing entry eligibility. The respondent argued that she was entitled to some explanation of the factual basis for the denial. The case produced no majority opinion. SCALIA, J., announced the judgment of the Court and issued an opinion in which Thomas, J., and Roberts, C.J., joined. He argued that there is no deeply rooted tradition protecting a citizen's right to live in the United States with her spouse and thus no fundamental right for substantive due process purposes. He then stated that absent the expression of a liberty interest in positive law such as a statute, the mere importance of an interest that is not otherwise fundamental for substantive due process purposes is insufficient to trigger procedural due process.

BREYER, J., opinion joined by Ginsburg, Sotomayor, and Kagan, JJ., dissented. He characterized prior cases as establishing that a liberty interest sufficient to trigger procedural due process protection may be established either by positive law or where the asserted liberty implicitly flows "from the design, object, and nature of the Due Process Clause." The dissenters thought that procedural due process entitled the respondent at least to "a statement of reasons, some kind of explanation."

KENNEDY, J., joined by Alito, J., assumed but did not decide that the respondent had invoked a sufficient liberty interest to trigger procedural due process but concluded that, in light of the national security concerns raised by visa decisions, the government's general citation of a Code section counted as sufficient notice: "Absent an affirmative showing of bad faith on the part of the consular officer who denied [the] visa—which Din has not plausibly alleged with sufficient particularity—*Kleindienst v. Mandel*, 408 US. 753 (1972), instructs us not to 'look behind' the Government's exclusion of" the noncitizen husband. The scope and meaning of "bad faith" could play a role in litigation challenging President Trump's executive order restricting entry into the country of nationals of six majority-Muslim countries. *See* Executive Order Protecting the Nation from Foreign Terrorists Entry Into the United States, https://www.whitehouse.gov/the-press-office/2017/03/06/executive-order-protecting-nation-foreign-terrorist-entry-united-states (Mar. 6, 2017, last visited June 15, 2017).

II. WHAT KIND OF HEARING—AND WHEN?

P. 634, at end of note 3:

NELSON v. COLORADO, 137 S.Ct. 1249 (2017), was a case brought by former prisoners whose convictions had been overturned. They challenged the State's procedure for obtaining a refund of costs, fees, and restitution they had been made to pay upon their initial convictions. According to the State, the *Eldridge* balancing test should not apply to their challenge because the claims concerned the operation of the criminal justice system. Thus, the State argued, no constitutional violation should be found unless the petitioners "were exposed to a procedure offensive to a fundamental principle of justice." The Court, per GINSBURG, J., disagreed that the State only needed to satisfy this forgiving standard: "Absent conviction of a crime, one is presumed innocent. Under the Colorado law before us in these cases, however, the State retains conviction-related assessments unless and until the prevailing defendant institutes a discrete civil proceeding and proves her innocence by clear and convincing evidence." Applying *Eldridge*, the Court concluded that "Colorado's scheme fails due process measurement because defendants' interest in regaining their funds is high, the risk of erroneous deprivation of those funds . . . is unacceptable, and the State has shown no countervailing interests in retaining the amounts in question."

ALITO, J., concurred only in the judgment because he thought that the less demanding "fundamental principle" standard applied but that the state procedure failed even this minimal test.

THOMAS, J., dissented on the ground that the petitioners lacked a property interest that triggered procedural protection. Under Colorado law, he said, the funds in question became state property once paid, and thus the petitioners could only establish a property interest in them by complying with the challenged state procedure.

CHAPTER 7

FREEDOM OF EXPRESSION AND ASSOCIATION

■ ■ ■

2. DISTINGUISHING BETWEEN CONTENT REGULATION AND MANNER REGULATION: UNCONVENTIONAL FORMS OF COMMUNICATION

P. 850, at end of note 3:

In HEFFERNAN v. CITY OF PATERSON, N.J., 136 S.Ct. 1412 (2016), the Court was called upon to confront directly the question whether an impermissible governmental motive was itself a violation of the First Amendment, even when no one had actually engaged in constitutionally protected activity. The facts were unusual, in that Heffernan, a police officer, claimed he had been demoted for engaging in partisan political activity despite the fact that his supervisors were mistaken in believing that he was in fact doing so. Heffernan was picking up and transporting a political sign for his mother, but witnesses and his supervisors believed, erroneously, that he himself was involved in the political campaign that had produced the sign. Relying on cases such as *Elrod v. Burns*, 427 U.S. 347 (1976), *Branti v. Finkel*, 445 U.S. 507 (1980), and *Rutan v. Republican Party of Illinois*, 497 U.S. 62 (1990), Heffernan claimed that he had been "deprived" of a "right . . . secured by the Constitution" in violation of 42 U.S.C. § 1983. In response, the city argued that because Heffernan was not actually engaged in political (or other First Amendment) activity, he had not been deprived of a constitutional right, and thus had no § 1983 claim.

Writing for the Court, BREYER, J., agreed with Heffernan that the state's impermissible motivation, by itself, constituted a violation of the First Amendment, and remanded for further determination below on the question of the actual reasons for Heffernan's dismissal. "We conclude that . . . the government's reason for demoting Heffernan is what counts here. When an employed demotes an employee out of a desire to prevent the employee from engaging in political activity that the First Amendment protects, the employee is entitled to challenge that unlawful action under the First Amendment and 42 U.S.C. § 1983—even if, as here, the employer makes a factual mistake about the employer's behavior." Because even a mistaken application of an impermissible motive would have the effect of discouraging constitutionally protected activity, Breyer argued, "a discharge or demotion based upon an

47

employer's belief that the employee has engaged in protected activity can cause the same kind, and degree, of constitutional harm whether that belief does or does not rest upon a factual mistake.

THOMAS, J., joined by Alito, J., dissented, arguing that a public employee does not have a cause of action for violating "a constitutional right that he concedes he did not exercise." Framing his dissent largely in terms of the necessary conditions for a § 1983 action, Justice Thomas insisted that "[a] city's policy, even if unconstitutional, cannot be the basis of a § 1983 suit when the policy does not result in the infringement of the plaintiff's constitutional rights."

3. IS SOME PROTECTED SPEECH LESS EQUAL THAN OTHER PROTECTED SPEECH?

II. COMMERCIAL SPEECH

P. 920, after note 5:

EXPRESSIONS HAIR DESIGN V. SCHNEIDERMAN
___ U.S. ___, 137 S.Ct. 1144, 197 L.Ed.2d 442 (2017).

CHIEF JUSTICE ROBERTS delivered the opinion of the Court.

Each time a customer pays for an item with a credit card, the merchant [must] pay a transaction fee to the credit card issuer. Some merchants balk at paying the fees and want to discourage the use of credit cards, or at least pass on the fees to customers who use them. One method of achieving those ends is through differential pricing—charging credit card users more than customers using cash. Merchants who wish to employ differential pricing may do so in two ways relevant here: impose a surcharge for the use of a credit card, or offer a discount for the use of cash. In N. Y. Gen. Bus. Law § 518, New York has banned the former practice. The question presented is whether § 518 regulates merchants' speech and—if so—whether the statute violates the First Amendment. We conclude that § 518 does regulate speech and remand for the Court of Appeals to determine in the first instance whether that regulation is unconstitutional.

I.A. When credit cards were first introduced, contracts between card issuers and merchants barred merchants from charging credit card users higher prices than cash customers. Congress put a partial stop to this practice in the 1974 amendments to the Truth in Lending Act (TILA). The amendments prohibited card issuers from contractually preventing merchants from giving discounts to customers who paid in cash. The law, however, said nothing about surcharges for the use of credit.

Two years later, Congress refined its dissimilar treatment of discounts and surcharges. First, the 1976 version of TILA barred merchants from imposing surcharges on customers who use credit cards. Second, Congress added definitions of the two terms. A discount was "a reduction made from the regular price," while a surcharge was "any means of increasing the regular price to a cardholder which is not imposed upon customers paying by cash, check, or similar means."

In 1981, Congress further delineated the distinction between discounts and surcharges by defining "regular price." Where a merchant "tagged or posted" a single price, the regular price was that single price. If no price was tagged or posted, or if a merchant employed a two-tag approach— posting one price for credit and another for cash—the regular price was whatever was charged to credit card users. Because a surcharge was defined as an increase from the regular price, there could be no credit card surcharge where the regular price was the same as the amount charged to customers using credit cards. [Thus] a merchant could violate the surcharge ban only by posting a single price and charging credit card users more than that posted price.

The federal surcharge ban was short lived. Congress allowed it to expire in 1984 and has not renewed the ban since. The provision preventing credit card issuers from contractually barring discounts for cash, however, remained in place. With the lapse of the federal surcharge ban, several States, New York among them, immediately enacted their own surcharge bans. Passed in 1984, N. Y. Gen. Bus. Law § 518 adopted the operative language of the federal ban verbatim, providing that "[n]o seller in any sales transaction may impose a surcharge on a holder who elects to use a credit card in lieu of payment by cash, check, or similar means." * * *

B. Petitioners, five New York businesses, [wish] to impose surcharges on customers who use credit cards. Each time one of their customers pays with a credit card, these merchants must pay some transaction fee to the company that issued the credit card. The fee is generally two to three percent of the purchase price. [Rather] than increase prices across the board to absorb those costs, the merchants want to pass the fees along only to their customers who choose to use credit cards. They also want to make clear that they are not the bad guys—that the credit card companies, not the merchants, are responsible for the higher prices.

[In] 2013, after several major credit card issuers agreed to drop their contractual surcharge prohibitions, the merchants filed suit [to] challenge § 518—the only remaining obstacle to their charging surcharges for credit card use. [They] argued that the law violated the First Amendment by regulating how they communicated their prices, and that it was unconstitutionally vague because liability under the law "turn[ed] on the blurry difference" between surcharges and discounts.

The District Court ruled in favor of the merchants. It read the statute as "draw[ing a] line between prohibited 'surcharges' and permissible 'discounts' based on words and labels, rather than economic realities." The court concluded that the law therefore regulated speech, and violated the First Amendment under this Court's commercial speech doctrine. [The] Court of Appeals for the Second Circuit vacated the judgment of the District Court with instructions to dismiss the merchants' claims. [All] the law did, [the] Court of Appeals explained, was regulate a relationship between two prices—the sticker price and the price charged to a credit card user—by requiring that the two prices be equal. Relying on our precedent holding that price regulation alone regulates conduct, not speech, the Court of Appeals concluded that § 518 did not violate the First Amendment.

II. [Although] the merchants have presented a wide array of hypothetical pricing regimes, they have expressly identified only one pricing scheme that they seek to employ: posting a cash price and an additional credit card surcharge, expressed either as a percentage surcharge or a "dollars-and-cents" additional amount. Under this pricing approach, petitioner Expressions Hair Design might, for example, post a sign outside its salon reading "Haircuts $10 (we add a 3% surcharge if you pay by credit card)." Or, petitioner Brooklyn Farmacy & Soda Fountain might list one of the sundaes on its menu as costing "$10 (with a $0.30 surcharge for credit card users)." We take petitioners at their word and limit our review to the question whether § 518 is unconstitutional as applied to this particular pricing practice.

III. The next question is whether § 518 prohibits the pricing regime petitioners wish to employ. The Court of Appeals concluded that it does. [We] follow that interpretation.

IV. A. The Court of Appeals concluded that § 518 posed no First Amendment problem because the law regulated conduct, not speech. [But] § 518 is not like a typical price regulation. Such a regulation—for example, a law requiring all New York delis to charge $10 for their sandwiches—would simply regulate the amount that a store could collect. In other words, it would regulate the sandwich seller's conduct. To be sure, in order to actually collect that money, a store would likely have to put "$10" on its menus or have its employees tell customers that price. Those written or oral communications would be speech, and the law—by determining the amount charged—would indirectly dictate the content of that speech. But the law's effect on speech would be only incidental to its primary effect on conduct, and "it has never been deemed an abridgment of freedom of speech or press to make a course of conduct illegal merely because the conduct was in part initiated, evidenced, or carried out by means of language, either spoken, written, or printed." *Rumsfeld v. Forum for Academic and Institutional Rights, Inc.*, 547 U. S. 47 (2006) (quoting *Giboney v. Empire Storage & Ice Co.*, 336 U. S. 490 (1949)).

Section 518 is different. The law tells merchants nothing about the amount they are allowed to collect from a cash or credit card payer. Sellers are free to charge $10 for cash and $9.70, $10, $10.30, or any other amount for credit. What the law does regulate is how sellers may communicate their prices. A merchant who wants to charge $10 for cash and $10.30 for credit may not convey that price any way he pleases. He is not free to say "$10, with a 3% credit card surcharge" or "$10, plus $0.30 for credit" because both of those displays identify a single sticker price—$10—that is less than the amount credit card users will be charged. Instead, if the merchant wishes to post a single sticker price, he must display $10.30 as his sticker price. Accordingly, while we agree with the Court of Appeals that § 518 regulates a relationship between a sticker price and the price charged to credit card users, we cannot accept its conclusion that § 518 is nothing more than a mine-run price regulation. In regulating the communication of prices rather than prices themselves, § 518 regulates speech.

Because it concluded otherwise, the Court of Appeals had no occasion to conduct a further inquiry into whether § 518, as a speech regulation, survived First Amendment scrutiny. On that question, the parties dispute whether § 518 is a valid commercial speech regulation under *Central Hudson*, and whether the law can be upheld as a valid disclosure requirement under *Zauderer* (sec. 9, infra).

"[W]e are a court of review, not of first view." *Nautilus, Inc. v. Biosig Instruments, Inc.*, 572 U. S. ___ (2014). Accordingly, we decline to consider those questions in the first instance. Instead, we remand for the Court of Appeals to analyze § 518 as a speech regulation. * * *

JUSTICE BREYER, concurring in the judgment.

I agree with the Court that New York's statute regulates speech. But that is because virtually all government regulation affects speech. Human relations take place through speech. And human relations include community activities of all kinds—commercial and otherwise.

When the government seeks to regulate those activities, it is often wiser not to try to distinguish between "speech" and "conduct." Instead, we can [simply] ask whether, or how, a challenged statute, rule, or regulation affects an interest that the First Amendment protects. If, for example, a challenged government regulation negatively affects the processes through which political discourse or public opinion is formed or expressed (interests close to the First Amendment's protective core), courts normally scrutinize that regulation with great care. *Boos v. Barry*, 485 U. S. 312 (1988). If the challenged regulation restricts the "informational function" provided by truthful commercial speech, courts will apply a "lesser" (but still elevated) form of scrutiny. *Central Hudson*. If, however, a challenged regulation simply requires a commercial speaker to disclose "purely factual and uncontroversial information," courts will apply a more permissive standard of review. *Zauderer.* Because that kind of regulation normally has only a "minimal" effect on First Amendment interests, it normally need only be "reasonably related to the State's interest in preventing deception of consumers." Courts apply a similarly permissive standard of review to "regulatory legislation affecting ordinary commercial transactions." *United States v. Carolene Products Co.* (ch. 5, sec. 3, supra). Since that legislation normally does not significantly affect the interests that the First Amendment protects, we normally look only for assurance that the legislation "rests upon some rational basis."

I repeat these well-known general standards or judicial approaches both because I believe that determining the proper approach is typically more important than trying to distinguish "speech" from "conduct," and because the parties here differ as to which approach applies. That difference reflects the fact that it is not clear just what New York's law does. On its face, the law seems simply to tell merchants that they cannot charge higher prices to credit-card users. If so, then it is an ordinary piece of commercial legislation subject to "rational basis" review. It may, however, make more sense to interpret the statute as working like the expired federal law that it replaced. If so, it would require a merchant, who posts prices and who wants to charge a higher credit-card price, simply to disclose that credit-card price. In that case, though affecting the merchant's "speech," it would not hinder the transmission of information to the public; the merchant would remain free to say whatever it wanted so long as it also revealed its credit-card price to customers. Accordingly, the law would still receive a deferential form of review.

[Because] the statute's operation is unclear and because its interpretation is a matter of state law, I agree with the majority that we should remand the case to the Second Circuit.

JUSTICE SOTOMAYOR, with whom JUSTICE ALITO joins, concurring in the judgment.

The Court addresses only one part of one half of petitioners' First Amendment challenge to the New York statute at issue here. This quarter-loaf outcome is worse than none. I would vacate the judgment below and remand with directions to certify the case to the New York Court of Appeals for a definitive interpretation of the statute that would permit the full resolution of petitioners' claims. I thus concur only in the judgment. . . .

SEC. 3

IS SOME PROTECTED SPEECH LESS EQUAL THAN
OTHER PROTECTED SPEECH?

53

IV. CONCEIVING AND RECONCEIVING THE STRUCTURE OF FIRST AMENDMENT DOCTRINE: HATE SPEECH REVISITED—AGAIN

P. 952, as new note 3:

3.   Although federal registration of a trademark is not strictly necessary for enforcement, registration provides the trademark registrant with remedies otherwise unavailable. Under 15 U.S.C. § 1052(a), however, the Patent and Trademark Office (PTO) may deny registration to any trademark that may "disparage . . . or bring . . . into contemp[t] or disrepute" any "persons, living or dead." Relying on this provision, the PTO denied trademark registration to a dance-rock band who wished to register the band's name—"The Slants." The band, whose members are Asian-Americans, used the name in an attempt to deprive the term of its traditional derogatory meaning as disparaging of those of Asian descent.

In MATAL v. TAM, 137 S.Ct. 1744 (2017), the Supreme Court unanimously held that § 1052's "disparagement clause" represented unconstitutional viewpoint discrimination. Announcing the judgment of the Court, ALITO, J. delivered an opinion that was unanimous in interpreting the disparagement clause's reference to "persons" as including the disparagement of racial or ethnic groups. And the opinion also represented the view of a unanimous Court in rejecting the argument that trademark registration was a form of government speech, thus making even viewpoint discrimination constitutionally permissible. (see infra, sec.7, and especially Walker v. Texas Division, Sons of Confederate Veterans, Inc., sec. 7, II, and Pleasant Grove City v. Summum, sec. 7, II). "[I]t is far-fetched to suggest that the content of a registered mark is government speech. [I]f trademarks represent government speech, what does the Government have in mind when it advises Americans to 'make.believe' (Sony), 'Think different' (Apple), 'Just do it' (Nike), or 'Have it your way' (Burger King)? [None] of our government speech cases even remotely supports the idea that registered trademarks are government speech."

Having concluded that trademarks are not government speech, Alito, now speaking only for himself, Roberts, CJ, and Thomas and Breyer, JJ, also concluded that trademark registration was neither the kind of government subsidy that might also be awarded on content- and viewpoint-based grounds (see Rust v. Sullivan, infra, sec. 7, II), nor the type of government program (see Davenport v. Washington Educ. Ass'n, infra, sec. 9, I) that may, again, be based on content or viewpoint. As a result of the inapplicability of none of these justifications for content- or viewpoint-discrimination, Alito found it unnecessary to address the question whether trademarks were commercial speech, because, he said, "the disparagement clause cannot withstand even Central Hudson (supra, sec. 3, II) review. [No] matter how the [government's] point is phrased, its unmistakable thrust is this: The Government has an interest in preventing speech expressing ideas that offend. And, as we have explained, that idea strikes at the heart of the First Amendment. Speech that demeans on the basis of race, ethnicity, gender, religion, age, disability, or any other similar ground is hateful; but the proudest boast of our free speech jurisprudence is that we protect the freedom to express the 'thought that we hate.' *United States v. Schwimmer*, 279 U.S. 644 (1929) (Holmes, J., dissenting). [We] hold that the disparagement clause violates the [First] Amendment."

Kennedy, J, writing for himself and Ginsburg, Sotomayor, and Kagan, JJ, agreed that "§ 1052(a) constitutes viewpoint discrimination—a form of speech suppression so potent that it must be subject to rigorous constitutional scrutiny. The Government's action and the statute on which it is based cannot survive this scrutiny. [The] test for viewpoint discrimination is whether—within the relevant subject category—the government has singled out a subset of messages for disfavor based on the views expressed. [Here] the law [reflects] the Government's disapproval of a subset of messages it finds offensive. This is the essence of viewpoint discrimination." Concluding that the "narrow" government speech and government program "exceptions" were inapplicable, and that even characterization of the speech as "commercial" "does not serve as a blanket exemption from the First Amendment's requirement of viewpoint neutrality," Kennedy concluded by joining the Court's opinion in part and concurring in the judgment. Thomas, J., also concurred in part and concurred in the judgment, joining all of Alito's opinion except for the part that dealt with the statutory interpretation argument, an argument Thomas believed was not properly before the Court. "I also write separately because 'I continue to believe that when the government seeks to restrict truthful speech in order to suppress the ideas it conveys, strict scrutiny is appropriate, whether or not the speech in question may be characterized as "commercial." ' " (Lorillard Tobacco Co. v. Reilly, supra, sec. 3, II (Thomas, J)).

———

Although it was "The Slants" case that reached the Supreme Court, prior attention to the issue of trademark registration of allegedly disparaging names had been focused on a challenge to the trademark registration of the Washington Redskins football team in the National Football League. See *Pro-Football, Inc. v. Blackhorse*, 112 F. Supp. 3d 439 (E.D. Va. 2015); *Pro-Football, Inc. v. Harjo*, 284 F. Supp. 2d 96 (D.D.C. 2003). See also Laura Sigler, Note, *The Saga Continues: The Redskins, Blackhorse, and the Future of Native American Trademarks in Sports*, 62 Wayne L. Rev. 73 (2016).

6. GOVERNMENT PROPERTY AND THE PUBLIC FORUM

II. NEW FORUMS

P. 1041, as new note 7:

7. Is all or part of social media a public forum for First Amendment purposes? In PACKINGHAM v. NORTH CAROLINA, 137 S.Ct. 1730 (2017), the Court addressed the question in the context of a North Carolina law making it a felony for a registered sex offender "to access a commercial social networking Web site where the sex offender knows that the site permits minor children to become members or to create or maintain personal Web pages." Lester Packingham was one of about 20,000 people in North Carolina to whom the statute applied, and one of over 1000 people prosecuted for violating it. He challenged the restriction on First Amendment grounds, and the Supreme Court, KENNEDY, J., writing for the majority, held the law, as written, to violate the First Amendment.

"A fundamental principle of the First Amendment is that all persons have access to places where they can speak and listen, and then, after reflection, speak and listen once more. The Court has sought to protect the right to speak in this spatial context. [While] in the past there may have been difficulty in identifying the most important places (in a spatial sense) for the exchange of views, today the answer is clear. It is cyberspace [in] general [and] social media in particular. [Social] media users employ [various] websites to engage in a wide array of protected First Amendment activity. [This] case is one of the first this Court has taken to address the relationship between the First Amendment and the modern Internet. As a result, the Court must exercise extreme caution before suggesting that the First Amendment provides scant protection for access to vast networks in that medium."

Against this background, the Court assumed that the statute was content neutral and thus to be evaluated according to "intermediate scrutiny." But even under this standard, the Court found the restriction excessively broad. "[To] foreclose access altogether is to prevent the user from engaging in the legitimate exercise of First Amendment rights. [Even] convicted criminals—and in some instances especially convicted criminals—might receive legitimate benefits from these means for access to the world of ideas . . . [The] analogy to this case is [Board of Airport Comm'rs of Los Angeles v. Jews for Jesus (supra, sec. 1, IV, C). [If] a law prohibiting 'all protected expression' at a single airport is not constitutional, it follows with even greater force that the State may not enact this complete bar to the exercise of First Amendment rights on websites integral to the fabric of our modern society and culture."

Concurring in the judgment, Alito, J., joined by Roberts, CJ, and Thomas, J, objected to what he called the Court's "undisciplined dicta." "The Court is unable to resist musings that seem to equate the entirety of the internet with public streets and parks." Finding it unnecessary to address the question of the nature of the internet as a public forum, or not, Alito still believed the North Carolina law unduly restrictive. "Because protecting children from abuse is a compelling state interest and sex offenders can (and do) use the internet to engage in such abuse, it is legitimate and entirely reasonable for states to try to stop abuse from occurring before it happens. [But the] fatal problem for [North Carolina's law] is that its wide sweep precludes access to a large number of websites that are most unlikely to facilitate the commission of a sex crime against a child." Using Amazon.com, washingtonpost.com, and WebMD as examples, Alito found invalid a law that prohibits registered sex offenders "from receiving or engaging in speech that the First Amendment protects and does not appreciably advance the State's goal of protecting children from recidivist sex offenders. [But] if the entirety of the internet or just 'social media' sites are the 21st century equivalent of public streets and parks, then [the Court's loose rhetoric . . . gives the States] little ability to restrict the sites that may be visited by even the most dangerous sex offenders. May a State preclude an adult previously convicted of molesting children from visiting a dating site for teenagers? Or a site where minors communicate with each other about personal problems? The Court should be more attentive to the implications of its rhetoric [because] there are important differences between cyberspace and the physical world."

III. PRIVACY AND THE PUBLIC FORUM

P. 1054, at end of Sec. 6:

REED V. GILBERT
___ U.S. ___, 135 S.Ct. 2218, 192 L.Ed.2d 236 (2015).

JUSTICE THOMAS delivered the opinion of the Court.

The town of Gilbert, Arizona (or Town), has adopted a comprehensive code governing the manner in which people may display outdoor signs. The Sign Code identifies various categories of signs based on the type of information they convey, then subjects each category to different restrictions. One of the categories is "Temporary Directional Signs Relating to a Qualifying Event," loosely defined as signs directing the public to a meeting of a nonprofit group. The Code imposes more stringent restrictions on these signs than it does on signs conveying other messages. We hold that these provisions are content-based regulations of speech that cannot survive strict scrutiny.

I.A. The Sign Code prohibits the display of outdoor signs anywhere within the Town without a permit, but it then exempts 23 categories of signs from that requirement. These exemptions include everything from bazaar signs to flying banners. Three categories of exempt signs are particularly relevant here.

The first is "Ideological Sign[s]." This category includes any "sign communicating a message or ideas for noncommercial purposes that is not a Construction Sign, Directional Sign, Temporary Directional Sign Relating to a Qualifying Event, Political Sign, Garage Sale Sign, or a sign owned or required by a governmental agency." Of the three categories discussed here, the Code treats ideological signs most favorably, allowing them to be up to 20 square feet in area and to be placed in all "zoning districts" without time limits.

The second category is "Political Sign[s]." This includes any "temporary sign designed to influence the outcome of an election called by a public body." The Code treats these signs less favorably than ideological signs. The Code allows the placement of political signs up to 16 square feet on residential property and up to 32 square feet on nonresidential property, undeveloped municipal property, and "rights-of-way." These signs may be displayed up to 60 days before a primary election and up to 15 days following a general election.

The third category is "Temporary Directional Signs Relating to a Qualifying Event." This includes any "Temporary Sign intended to direct pedestrians, motorists, and other passersby to a 'qualifying event.'" A "qualifying event" is defined as any "assembly, gathering, activity, or meeting sponsored, arranged, or promoted by a religious, charitable, community service, educational, or other similar non-profit organization." The Code treats temporary directional signs even less favorably than political signs. Temporary directional signs may be no larger than six square feet. They may be placed on private property or on a public right-of-way, but no more than four signs may be placed on a single property at any time. And, they may be displayed no more than 12 hours before the "qualifying event" and no more than 1 hour afterward.

B.   Petitioners Good News Community Church and its pastor [wish] to advertise the time and location of their Sunday church services. The Church is a small, cash-strapped entity that owns no building, so it holds its services at elementary schools or other locations in or near the Town. In order to inform the public about its services, which are held in a variety of different locations, the Church began placing 15 to 20 temporary signs around the Town, frequently in the public right-of-way abutting the street. The signs typically displayed the Church's name, along with the time and location of the upcoming service. Church members would post the signs early in the day on Saturday and then remove them around midday on Sunday. The display of these signs requires little money and manpower, and thus has proved to be an economical and effective way for the Church to let the community know where its services are being held each week.

This practice caught the attention of the Town's Sign Code compliance manager, who twice cited the Church for violating the Code. The first citation noted that the Church exceeded the time limits for displaying its temporary directional signs. The second citation referred to the same problem, along with the Church's failure to include the date of the event on the signs. [Pastor] Reed contacted the Sign Code Compliance Department in an attempt to reach an accommodation. His efforts proved unsuccessful. Shortly thereafter, petitioners filed a complaint in the United States District Court for the District of Arizona, arguing that the Sign Code abridged their freedom of speech. [The] District Court denied the petitioners' motion for a preliminary injunction. The Court of Appeals for the Ninth Circuit affirmed, holding that the Sign Code's provision regulating temporary directional signs did not regulate speech on the basis of content. [It] then remanded for the District Court to determine in the first instance whether the Sign Code's distinctions among temporary directional signs, political signs, and ideological signs nevertheless constituted a content-based regulation of speech. On remand, the District Court granted summary judgment in favor of the Town. The Court of Appeals again affirmed, holding that the Code's sign categories were content neutral. We granted certiorari, and now reverse.

II.A.   Under [the Free Speech Clause], a government, including a municipal government vested with state authority, "has no power to restrict expression because of its message, its ideas, its subject matter, or its content." [Mosley] Content-based laws—those that target speech based on its communicative content—are presumptively unconstitutional and may be justified only if the government proves that they are narrowly tailored to serve compelling state interests. [R.A.V.]

Government regulation of speech is content based if a law applies to particular speech because of the topic discussed or the idea or message expressed. This commonsense meaning of the phrase "content based" requires a court to consider whether a regulation of speech "on its face" draws distinctions based on the message a speaker conveys. Some facial distinctions based on a message are obvious, defining regulated speech by particular subject matter, and others are more subtle, defining regulated speech by its function or purpose. Both are distinctions drawn based on the message a speaker conveys, and, therefore, are subject to strict scrutiny.

Our precedents have also recognized a separate and additional category of laws that, though facially content neutral, will be considered content-based regulations of speech: laws that cannot be " 'justified without reference to the content of the regulated speech,' " or that were adopted by the government "because of disagreement with the message [the speech] conveys." Those laws, like those that are content based on their face, must also satisfy strict scrutiny.

B.   The Town's Sign Code is content based on its face. It defines "Temporary Directional Signs" on the basis of whether a sign conveys the message of directing the public to church or some other "qualifying event." It defines "Political Signs" on the basis of whether a sign's message is "designed to influence the outcome of an election." And it defines "Ideological Signs" on the basis of whether a sign "communicat[es] a message or ideas" that do not fit within the Code's other categories. It then subjects each of these categories to different restrictions.

The restrictions in the Sign Code that apply to any given sign thus depend entirely on the communicative content of the sign. If a sign informs its reader of the time and place a book club will discuss John Locke's Two Treatises of Government, that sign will be treated differently from a sign expressing the view that one should vote for one of Locke's followers in an upcoming election, and both signs will be treated differently from a sign expressing an ideological view rooted in Locke's theory of government. More to the point, the Church's signs inviting people to attend its worship services are treated differently from signs conveying other types of ideas. On its face, the Sign Code is a content-based regulation of speech. We thus have no need to consider the government's justifications or purposes for enacting the Code to determine whether it is subject to strict scrutiny.

C.　In reaching the contrary conclusion, the Court of Appeals offered several theories to explain why the Town's Sign Code should be deemed content neutral. None is persuasive.

1.　The Court of Appeals first determined that the Sign Code was content neutral because the Town "did not adopt its regulation of speech [based on] disagree[ment] with the message conveyed," and its justifications for regulating temporary directional signs were "unrelated to the content of the sign." In its brief to this Court, the United States similarly contends that a sign regulation is content neutral—even if it expressly draws distinctions based on the sign's communicative content— if those distinctions can be " 'justified without reference to the content of the regulated speech.' But this analysis skips the crucial first step in the content-neutrality analysis: determining whether the law is content neutral on its face. A law that is content based on its face is subject to strict scrutiny regardless of the government's benign motive, content-neutral justification, or lack of "animus toward the ideas contained" in the regulated speech. We have thus made clear that " '[i]llicit legislative intent is not the sine qua non of a violation of the First Amendment,' " and a party opposing the government "need adduce 'no evidence of an improper censorial motive.' " Although "a content-based purpose may be sufficient in certain circumstances to show that a regulation is content based, it is not necessary. In other words, an innocuous justification cannot transform a facially content-based law into one that is content neutral.

That is why we have repeatedly considered whether a law is content neutral on its face *before* turning to the law's justification or purpose.

Because strict scrutiny applies either when a law is content based on its face or when the purpose and justification for the law are content based, a court must evaluate each question before it concludes that the law is content neutral and thus subject to a lower level of scrutiny. [Innocent] motives do not eliminate the danger of censorship presented by a facially content-based statute, as future government officials may one day wield such statutes to suppress disfavored speech. That is why the First Amendment expressly targets the operation of the laws—*i.e.,* the "abridg[ement] of speech"—rather than merely the motives of those who enacted them. [One] could easily imagine a Sign Code compliance manager who disliked the Church's substantive teachings deploying the Sign Code to make it more difficult for the Church to inform the public of the location of its services. Accordingly, we have repeatedly "rejected the argument that 'discriminatory . . . treatment is suspect under the First Amendment only when the legislature intends to suppress certain ideas.' " We do so again today.

2. The Court of Appeals next reasoned that the Sign Code was content neutral because it "does not mention any idea or viewpoint, let alone single one out for differential treatment." It reasoned that, for the purpose of the Code provisions, "[i]t makes no difference which candidate is supported, who sponsors the event, or what ideological perspective is asserted." The Town seizes on this reasoning, insisting that "content based" is a term of art that "should be applied flexibly" with the goal of protecting "viewpoints and ideas from government censorship or favoritism." In the Town's view, a sign regulation that "does not censor or favor particular viewpoints or ideas" cannot be content based. The Sign Code allegedly passes this test because its treatment of temporary directional signs does not raise any concerns that the government is "endorsing or suppressing 'ideas or viewpoints,' " and the provisions for political signs and ideological signs "are neutral as to particular ideas or viewpoints" within those categories.

This analysis conflates two distinct but related limitations that the First Amendment places on government regulation of speech. Government discrimination among viewpoints—or the regulation of speech based on "the specific motivating ideology or the opinion or perspective of the speaker"—is a "more blatant" and "egregious form of content discrimination." But it is well established that "[t]he First Amendment's hostility to content-based regulation extends not only to restrictions on particular viewpoints, but also to prohibition of public discussion of an entire topic."

Thus, a speech regulation targeted at specific subject matter is content based even if it does not discriminate among viewpoints within that subject matter. For example, a law banning the use of sound trucks for political speech—and only political speech—would be a content-based regulation, even if it imposed no limits on the political viewpoints that could be expressed. The Town's Sign Code likewise singles out specific subject matter for differential treatment, even if it does not target viewpoints within that subject matter. Ideological messages are given more favorable treatment than messages concerning a political candidate, which are themselves given more favorable treatment than messages announcing an assembly of like-minded individuals. That is a paradigmatic example of content-based discrimination.

3. Finally, the Court of Appeals characterized the Sign Code's distinctions as turning on " 'the content-neutral elements of who is speaking through the sign and whether and when an event is occurring.' " That analysis is mistaken on both factual and legal grounds.

To start, the Sign Code's distinctions are not speaker based. The restrictions for political, ideological, and temporary event signs apply equally no matter who sponsors them. If a local business, for example, sought to put up signs advertising the Church's meetings, those signs would be subject to the same limitations as such signs placed by the Church. And if Reed had decided to display signs in support of a particular candidate, he could have made those signs far larger—and kept them up for far longer—than signs inviting people to attend his church services. If the Code's distinctions were truly speaker based, both types of signs would receive the same treatment.

In any case, the fact that a distinction is speaker based does not, as the Court of Appeals seemed to believe, automatically render the distinction content neutral. Because "[s]peech restrictions based on the identity of the speaker are all too often simply a means to control content," [Citizens United, infra] we have insisted that "laws favoring some speakers over others demand strict scrutiny when the legislature's speaker preference reflects a content preference." Thus, a law limiting the content of newspapers, but only newspapers, could not evade strict scrutiny simply because it could be characterized as speaker based. Likewise, a content-based law that restricted the political speech of all corporations would not become content neutral just because it singled out corporations as a class of speakers. Characterizing a distinction as speaker based is only the beginning—not the end—of the inquiry.

[As] with speaker-based laws, the fact that a distinction is event based does not render it content neutral. The Court of Appeals cited no precedent from this Court supporting its novel theory of an exception from the content-neutrality requirement for event-based laws. As we have explained, a speech regulation is content based if the law applies to particular speech because of the topic discussed or the idea or message expressed. A regulation that targets a sign because it conveys an idea about a specific event is no less content based than a regulation that targets a sign because it conveys some other idea. Here, the Code singles out signs bearing a particular message: the time and location of a specific event. This type of ordinance may seem like a perfectly rational way to regulate signs, but a clear and firm rule governing content neutrality is an essential means of protecting the freedom of speech, even if laws that might seem "entirely reasonable" will sometimes be "struck down because of their content-based nature."

III. Because the Town's Sign Code imposes content-based restrictions on speech, those provisions can stand only if they survive strict scrutiny. [Thus,] it is the Town's burden to demonstrate that the Code's differentiation between temporary directional signs and other types of signs, such as political signs and ideological signs, furthers a compelling governmental interest and is narrowly tailored to that end.

The Town cannot do so. It has offered only two governmental interests in support of the distinctions the Sign Code draws: preserving the Town's aesthetic appeal and traffic safety. Assuming for the sake of argument that those are compelling governmental interests, the Code's distinctions fail as hopelessly underinclusive.

Starting with the preservation of aesthetics, temporary directional signs are "no greater an eyesore," than ideological or political ones. Yet the Code allows unlimited proliferation of larger ideological signs while strictly limiting the number, size, and duration of smaller directional ones. The Town cannot claim that placing strict limits on temporary directional signs is necessary to beautify the Town while at the same time allowing unlimited numbers of other types of signs that create the same problem.

The Town similarly has not shown that limiting temporary directional signs is necessary to eliminate threats to traffic safety, but that limiting other types of signs is not. The Town has offered no reason to believe that directional signs pose a greater threat to safety than do ideological or political signs. If anything, a sharply worded ideological sign seems more likely to distract a driver than a sign directing the public to a nearby church meeting.

In light of this underinclusiveness, the Town has not met its burden to prove that its Sign Code is narrowly tailored to further a compelling government interest. Because a " 'law cannot be regarded as protecting an interest of the highest order, and thus as justifying a restriction on truthful speech, when it leaves appreciable damage to that supposedly vital interest unprohibited,' " the Sign Code fails strict scrutiny.

IV. Our decision today will not prevent governments from enacting effective sign laws. The Town asserts that an " 'absolutist' " content-neutrality rule would render "virtually all distinctions in sign laws . . . subject to strict scrutiny," but that is not the case. Not "all distinctions" are subject to strict scrutiny, only *content-based* ones are. Laws that are *content neutral* are instead subject to lesser scrutiny.

The Town has ample content-neutral options available to resolve problems with safety and aesthetics. For example, its current Code regulates many aspects of signs that have nothing to do with a sign's message: size, building materials, lighting, moving parts, and portability. And on public property, the Town may go a long way toward entirely forbidding the posting of signs, so long as it does so in an evenhanded, content-neutral manner. * * * We acknowledge that a city might reasonably view the general regulation of signs as necessary because signs "take up space and may obstruct views, distract motorists, displace alternative uses for land, and pose other problems that legitimately call for regulation. At the same time, the presence of certain signs may be essential, both for vehicles and pedestrians, to guide traffic or to identify hazards and ensure safety. A sign ordinance narrowly tailored to the challenges of protecting the safety of pedestrians, drivers, and passengers—such as warning signs marking hazards on private property, signs directing traffic, or street numbers associated with private houses— well might survive strict scrutiny. The signs at issue in this case, including political and ideological signs and signs for events, are far removed from those purposes. As discussed above, they are facially content based and are neither justified by traditional safety concerns nor narrowly tailored.

We reverse the judgment of the Court of Appeals and remand the case for proceedings consistent with this opinion.

JUSTICE ALITO, with whom JUSTICE KENNEDY and JUSTICE SOTOMAYOR join, concurring.

I join the opinion of the Court but add a few words of further explanation.

As the Court holds, what we have termed "content-based" laws must satisfy strict scrutiny. Content-based laws merit this protection because they present, albeit sometimes in a subtler form, the same dangers as laws that regulate speech based on viewpoint. Limiting speech based on its "topic" or "subject" favors those who do not want to disturb the status quo. Such regulations may interfere with democratic self-government and the search for truth.

As the Court shows, the regulations at issue in this case are replete with content-based distinctions, and as a result they must satisfy strict scrutiny. This does not mean, however, that municipalities are powerless to enact and enforce reasonable sign regulations. I will not attempt to provide anything like a comprehensive list, but here are some rules that would not be content based:

Rules regulating the size of signs. These rules may distinguish among signs based on any content-neutral criteria, including any relevant criteria listed below.

Rules regulating the locations in which signs may be placed. These rules may distinguish between free-standing signs and those attached to buildings.

Rules distinguishing between lighted and unlighted signs.

Rules distinguishing between signs with fixed messages and electronic signs with messages that change.

Rules that distinguish between the placement of signs on private and public property.

Rules distinguishing between the placement of signs on commercial and residential property.

Rules distinguishing between on-premises and off-premises signs.

Rules restricting the total number of signs allowed per mile of roadway.

Rules imposing time restrictions on signs advertising a one-time event. Rules of this nature do not discriminate based on topic or subject and are akin to rules restricting the times within which oral speech or music is allowed.

[Properly] understood, today's decision will not prevent cities from regulating signs in a way that fully protects public safety and serves legitimate esthetic objectives.

JUSTICE BREYER, concurring in the judgment.

I join JUSTICE KAGAN's separate opinion.

[Content] discrimination, while helping courts to identify unconstitutional suppression of expression, cannot and should not *always* trigger strict scrutiny. To say that it is not an automatic "strict scrutiny" trigger is not to argue against that concept's use. I readily concede, for example, that content discrimination, as a conceptual tool, can sometimes reveal weaknesses in the government's rationale for a rule that limits speech. If, for example, a city looks to litter prevention as the rationale for a prohibition against placing newsracks dispensing free advertisements on public property, why does it exempt other newsracks causing similar litter? I also concede that, whenever government disfavors one kind of speech, it places that speech at a disadvantage, potentially interfering with the free marketplace of ideas and with an individual's ability to express thoughts and ideas that can help that individual determine the kind of society in which he wishes to live, help shape that society, and help define his place within it.

Nonetheless, in these latter instances to use the presence of content discrimination automatically to trigger strict scrutiny and thereby call into play a strong presumption against constitutionality goes too far. That is because virtually all government activities involve speech, many of which involve the regulation of speech. Regulatory programs almost always require content discrimination. And to hold that such content discrimination triggers strict scrutiny is to write a recipe for judicial management of ordinary government regulatory activity.

Consider a few examples of speech regulated by government that inevitably involve content discrimination, but where a strong presumption against constitutionality has no place. Consider governmental regulation of securities, (e.g., requirements for content that must be included in a registration statement); of energy conservation labeling-practices (requirements for content that must be included on labels of certain consumer electronics); of prescription drugs, (requiring a prescription drug label to bear the symbol "Rx only"); of doctor-patient confidentiality, (requiring confidentiality of certain medical records, but allowing a physician to disclose that the patient has HIV to the patient's spouse or sexual partner); of income tax statements, (requiring taxpayers to furnish information about foreign gifts received if the aggregate amount exceeds $10,000); of commercial airplane briefings, (requiring pilots to ensure that each passenger has been briefed on flight procedures, such as seatbelt fastening); of signs at petting zoos, e.g., N.Y. Gen. Bus. Law Ann. § 399– ff(3) (West Cum. Supp. 2015) (requiring petting zoos to post a sign at every exit " 'strongly recommend[ing] that persons wash their hands upon exiting the petting zoo area' "); and so on.

[I] recognize that the Court could escape the problem by watering down the force of the presumption against constitutionality that "strict scrutiny" normally carries with it. But, in my view, doing so will weaken the First Amendment's protection in instances where "strict scrutiny" should apply in full force.

The better approach is to generally treat content discrimination as a strong reason weighing against the constitutionality of a rule where a traditional public forum, or where viewpoint discrimination, is threatened, but elsewhere treat it as a rule of thumb, finding it a helpful, but not determinative legal tool, in an appropriate case, to determine the strength of a justification. I would use content discrimination as a supplement to a more basic analysis, which, tracking most of our First Amendment cases, asks whether the regulation at issue works harm to First Amendment interests that is disproportionate in light of the relevant regulatory objectives. Answering this question requires examining the seriousness of the harm to speech, the importance of the countervailing objectives, the extent to which the law will achieve those objectives, and whether there are other, less restrictive ways of doing so. Admittedly, this approach does not have the simplicity of a mechanical use of categories. But it does permit the government to regulate speech in numerous instances where the voters have authorized the government to regulate and where courts should hesitate to substitute judicial judgment for that of administrators.

Here, regulation of signage along the roadside, for purposes of safety and beautification is at issue. There is no traditional public forum nor do I find any general effort to censor a particular viewpoint. Consequently, the specific regulation at issue does not warrant "strict scrutiny." Nonetheless, for the reasons that Justice Kagan sets forth, I believe that the Town of Gilbert's regulatory rules violate the First Amendment. I consequently concur in the Court's judgment only.

JUSTICE KAGAN, with whom JUSTICE GINSBURG and JUSTICE BREYER join, concurring in the judgment.

Countless cities and towns across America have adopted ordinances regulating the posting of signs, while exempting certain categories of signs based on their subject matter. For example, some municipalities generally prohibit illuminated signs in residential neighborhoods, but lift that ban for signs that identify the address of a home or the name of its owner or occupant. In other municipalities, safety signs such as "Blind Pedestrian Crossing" and "Hidden Driveway" can be posted without a permit, even as other permanent signs require one. Elsewhere, historic site markers—for example, "George Washington Slept Here"—are also exempt from general regulations. And similarly, the federal Highway Beautification Act limits signs along interstate highways unless, for instance, they direct travelers to "scenic and historical attractions" or advertise free coffee.

Given the Court's analysis, many sign ordinances of that kind are now in jeopardy. [And] although the majority holds out hope that some sign laws with subject-matter exemptions "might survive" that stringent review, the likelihood is that most will be struck down. After all, it is the "rare case[ ] in which a speech restriction withstands strict scrutiny." [Williams-Yulee, infra]. To clear that high bar, the government must show that a content-based distinction "is necessary to serve a compelling state interest and is narrowly drawn to achieve that end." So on the majority's view, courts would have to determine that a town has a compelling interest in informing passersby where George Washington slept. And likewise, courts would have to find that a town has no other way to prevent hidden-driveway mishaps than by specially treating hidden-driveway signs. (Well-placed speed bumps? Lower speed limits? Or how about just a ban on hidden driveways?) The consequence—unless courts water down strict scrutiny to something unrecognizable—is that our communities will find themselves in an unenviable bind: They will have to either repeal the exemptions that allow for helpful signs on streets and sidewalks, or else lift their sign restrictions altogether and resign themselves to the resulting clutter.

Although the majority insists that applying strict scrutiny to all such ordinances is "essential" to protecting First Amendment freedoms, I find it challenging to understand why that is so. This Court's decisions articulate two important and related reasons for subjecting content-based speech regulations to the most exacting standard of review. The first is "to preserve an uninhibited marketplace of ideas in which truth will ultimately prevail." The second is to ensure that the government has not regulated speech "based on hostility—or favoritism—towards the underlying message expressed." Yet the subject-matter exemptions included in many sign ordinances do not implicate those concerns. Allowing residents, say, to install a light bulb over "name and address" signs but no others does not distort the marketplace of ideas. Nor does that different treatment give rise to an inference of impermissible government motive.

We apply strict scrutiny to facially content-based regulations of speech, in keeping with the rationales just described, when there is any "realistic possibility that official suppression of ideas is afoot." That is always the case when the regulation facially differentiates on the basis of viewpoint. It is also the case (except in non-public or limited public forums) when a law restricts "discussion of an entire topic" in public debate. We have stated that "[i]f the marketplace of ideas is to remain free and open, governments must not be allowed to choose 'which issues are worth discussing or debating.' " And we have recognized that such subject-matter restrictions, even though viewpoint-neutral on their face, may "suggest[ ] an attempt to give one side of a debatable public question an advantage in expressing its views to the people." Subject-matter regulation, in other words, may have the intent or effect of favoring some ideas over others. When that is realistically possible—when the restriction "raises the specter that the Government may effectively drive certain ideas or viewpoints from the marketplace"—we insist that the law pass the most demanding constitutional scrutiny. But when that is not realistically possible, we may do well to relax our guard so that "entirely reasonable" laws imperiled by strict scrutiny can survive. This point is by no means new. Our concern with content-based regulation arises from the fear that the government will skew the public's debate of ideas—so when "that risk is inconsequential, . . . strict scrutiny is unwarranted." To do its intended work, of course, the category of content-based regulation triggering strict scrutiny must sweep more broadly than the actual harm; that category exists to create a buffer zone guaranteeing that the government cannot favor or disfavor certain viewpoints. But that buffer zone need not extend forever. We can administer our content-regulation doctrine with a dose of common sense, so as to leave standing laws that in no way implicate its intended function.

And indeed we have done just that: Our cases have been far less rigid than the majority admits in applying strict scrutiny to facially content-based laws—including in cases just like this one. [In *Ladue v. Gilleo*,] the Court assumed *arguendo* that a sign ordinance's exceptions for address signs, safety signs, and for-sale signs in residential areas did not trigger strict scrutiny. We did not need to, and so did not, decide the level-of-scrutiny question because the law's breadth made it unconstitutional under any standard.

The majority could easily have taken *Ladue*'s tack here. The Town of Gilbert's defense of its sign ordinance—most notably, the law's distinctions between directional signs and others—does not pass strict scrutiny, or intermediate scrutiny, or even the laugh test. The Town, for example, provides no reason at all for prohibiting more than four directional signs on a property while placing no limits on the number of other types of signs. Similarly, the Town offers no coherent justification for restricting the size of directional signs to 6 square feet while allowing other signs to reach 20 square feet. The best the Town could come up with at oral argument was that directional signs "need to be smaller because they need to guide travelers along a route." Why exactly a smaller sign better helps travelers get to where they are going is left a mystery. The absence of any sensible basis for these and other distinctions dooms the Town's ordinance under even the intermediate scrutiny that the Court typically applies to "time, place, or manner" speech regulations. Accordingly, there is no need to decide in this case whether strict scrutiny applies to every sign ordinance in every town across this country containing a subject-matter exemption.

I suspect this Court and others will regret the majority's insistence today on answering that question in the affirmative. As the years go by, courts will discover that thousands of towns have such ordinances, many of them "entirely reasonable." And as the challenges to them mount, courts will have to invalidate one after the other. (This Court may soon find itself a veritable Supreme Board of Sign Review.) And courts will strike down those democratically enacted local laws even though no one—certainly not the majority—has ever explained why the vindication of First Amendment values requires that result. Because I see no reason why such an easy case calls for us to cast a constitutional pall on reasonable regulations quite unlike the law before us, I concur only in the judgment.

7. GOVERNMENT SPEECH

I. SUBSIDIES OF SPEECH

P. 1069, after note 7:

WALKER v. TEXAS DIVISION, SONS OF CONFEDERATE VETERANS, INC.
___ U.S. ___, 135 S.Ct. 2239, 192 L.Ed.2d 274 (2015).

JUSTICE BREYER delivered the opinion of the Court.

Texas offers automobile owners a choice between ordinary and specialty license plates. Those who want the State to issue a particular specialty plate may propose a plate design, comprising a slogan, a graphic, or (most commonly) both. If the Department of Motor Vehicles Board approves the design, the State will make it available for display on vehicles registered in Texas.

In this case, the Texas Division of the Sons of Confederate Veterans proposed a specialty license plate design featuring a Confederate battle flag. The Board rejected the proposal. We must decide whether that rejection violated the Constitution's free speech guarantees. We conclude that it did not.

I.   A. Texas law requires all motor vehicles operating on the State's roads to display valid license plates. And Texas makes available several kinds of plates. Drivers may choose to display the State's general-issue license plates. Each of these plates contains the word "Texas," a license plate number, a silhouette of the State, a graphic of the Lone Star, and the slogan "The Lone Star State." In the alternative, drivers may choose from an assortment of specialty license plates. Each of these plates contains the word "Texas," a license plate number, and one of a selection of designs prepared by the State. Finally, Texas law provides for personalized plates (also known as "vanity plates"). Pursuant to the personalization program, a vehicle owner may request a particular alphanumeric pattern for use as a plate number, such as "BOB" or "TEXPL8." Here we are concerned only with the second category of plates, namely specialty license plates, not with the personalization program. Texas offers vehicle owners a variety of specialty plates, generally for an annual fee. And Texas selects the designs for specialty plates through three distinct processes.

First, the state legislature may specifically call for the development of a specialty license plate. The legislature has enacted statutes authorizing, for example, plates that say "Keep Texas Beautiful" and "Mothers Against Drunk Driving," plates that "honor" the Texas citrus industry, and plates that feature an image of the World Trade Center towers and the words "Fight Terrorism." Second, the Board may approve a specialty plate design proposal that a state-designated private vendor has created at the request of an individual or organization. Among the plates created through the private-vendor process are plates promoting the "Keller Indians" and plates with the slogan "Get it Sold with RE/MAX." Third, the Board "may create new specialty license plates on its own initiative or on receipt of an application from a" nonprofit entity seeking to sponsor a specialty plate. A nonprofit must include in its application "a draft design of the specialty license plate." And Texas law vests in the Board authority to approve or to disapprove an application. The relevant statute says that the Board "may refuse to create a new specialty license plate" for a number of reasons, for example "if the design might be offensive to any member of the public . . . or for any other reason established by rule." Specialty plates that the Board has sanctioned through this process include plates featuring the words "The Gator Nation," together with the Florida Gators logo, and plates featuring the logo of Rotary International and the words "SERVICE ABOVE SELF."

B.   In 2009, the Sons of Confederate Veterans, Texas Division (a nonprofit entity), applied to sponsor a specialty license plate through this last-mentioned process. [At] the bottom of the proposed plate were the words "SONS OF CONFEDERATE VETERANS." At the side was the organization's logo, a square Confederate battle flag framed by the words "Sons of Confederate Veterans 1896." A faint Confederate battle flag appeared in the background on the lower portion of the plate. [In] the middle of the plate was the license plate number, and at the top was the State's name and silhouette. The Board's predecessor denied this application.

In 2010, SCV renewed its application before the Board. The Board invited public comment on its website and at an open meeting. After considering the responses, including a number of letters sent by elected officials who opposed the proposal, the Board voted unanimously against issuing the plate. The Board explained that it had found "it necessary to deny th[e] plate design application, specifically the confederate flag portion of the design, because public comments ha[d] shown that many members of the general public find the design offensive, and because such comments are reasonable." The Board added "that a significant portion of the public associate the confederate flag with organizations advocating expressions of hate directed toward people or groups that is demeaning to those people or groups."

In 2012, SCV [brought] this lawsuit, [arguing] that the Board's decision violated the Free Speech Clause of the First Amendment. [The] District Court entered judgment for the Board. A divided panel of the Court of Appeals for the Fifth Circuit reversed. It held that Texas's specialty license plate designs are private speech and that the Board, in refusing to approve SCV's design, engaged in constitutionally forbidden viewpoint discrimination. The dissenting judge argued that Texas's specialty license plate designs are government speech, the content of which the State is free to control.

We granted the Board's petition for certiorari, and we now reverse.

II. When government speaks, it is not barred by the Free Speech Clause from determining the content of what it says. [*Summum*]. That freedom in part reflects the fact that it is the democratic electoral process that first and foremost provides a check on government speech. Thus, government statements (and government actions and programs that take the form of speech) do not normally trigger the First Amendment rules designed to protect the marketplace of ideas. Instead, the Free Speech Clause helps produce informed opinions among members of the public, who are then able to influence the choices of a government that, through words and deeds, will reflect its electoral mandate.

Were the Free Speech Clause interpreted otherwise, government would not work. How could a city government create a successful recycling program if officials, when writing householders asking them to recycle cans and bottles, had to include in the letter a long plea from the local trash disposal enterprise demanding the contrary? How could a state government effectively develop programs designed to encourage and provide vaccinations, if officials also had to voice the perspective of those who oppose this type of immunization? "[I]t is not easy to imagine how government could function if it lacked th[e] freedom" to select the messages it wishes to convey [*Summum*].

We have therefore refused "[t]o hold that the Government unconstitutionally discriminates on the basis of viewpoint when it chooses to fund a program dedicated to advance certain permissible goals, because the program in advancing those goals necessarily discourages alternative goals." [Rust v. Sullivan]. We have pointed out that a contrary holding "would render numerous Government programs constitutionally suspect." And we have made clear that "the government can speak for itself."

That is not to say that a government's ability to express itself is without restriction. Constitutional and statutory provisions outside of the Free Speech Clause may limit government speech. And the Free Speech Clause itself may constrain the government's speech if, for example, the government seeks to compel private persons to convey the government's speech. But, as a general matter, when the government speaks it is entitled to promote a program, to espouse a policy, or to take a position. * * *

III. In our view, specialty license plates issued pursuant to Texas's statutory scheme convey government speech. Our reasoning rests primarily on our analysis in *Summum*. [We] conclude here, as we did there, that our precedents regarding government speech (and not our precedents regarding forums for private speech) provide the appropriate framework through which to approach the case.

A. In *Summum,* we [held that] the speech at issue [was] "best viewed as a form of government speech" and "therefore [was] not subject to scrutiny under the Free Speech Clause." * * *

B. Our analysis in *Summum* leads us to the conclusion that here, too, government speech is at issue. First, the history of license plates shows that, insofar as license plates have conveyed more than state names and vehicle identification numbers, they long have communicated messages from the States. In 1917, Arizona became the first State to display a graphic on its plates. The State presented a depiction of the head of a Hereford steer. In the years since, New Hampshire plates have featured the profile of the "Old Man of the Mountain," Massachusetts plates have included a representation of the Commonwealth's famous codfish, and Wyoming plates have displayed a rider atop a bucking bronco.

In 1928, Idaho became the first State to include a slogan on its plates. The 1928 Idaho plate proclaimed "Idaho Potatoes" and featured an illustration of a brown potato, onto which the license plate number was superimposed in green. The brown potato did not catch on, but slogans on license plates did. Over the years, state plates have included the phrases "North to the Future" (Alaska), "Keep Florida Green" (Florida), "Hoosier Hospitality" (Indiana), "The Iodine Products State" (South Carolina), "Green Mountains" (Vermont), and "America's Dairyland" (Wisconsin). States have used license plate slogans to urge action, to promote tourism, and to tout local industries.

Texas, too, has selected various messages to communicate through its license plate designs. By 1919, Texas had begun to display the Lone Star emblem on its plates. In 1936, the State's general-issue plates featured the first slogan on Texas license plates: the word "Centennial." In 1968, Texas plates promoted a San Antonio event by including the phrase "Hemisfair 68." [And] in 1995, Texas plates celebrated "150 Years of Statehood." Additionally, the Texas Legislature has specifically authorized specialty plate designs stating, among other things, "Read to Succeed," "Houston Livestock Show and Rodeo," "Texans Conquer Cancer," and "Girl Scouts." * * *

[Texas] license plate designs "are often closely identified in the public mind with the [State]." Each Texas license plate is a government article serving the governmental purposes of vehicle registration and identification. The governmental nature of the plates is clear from their faces: The State places the name "TEXAS" in large letters at the top of every plate. Moreover, the State requires Texas vehicle owners to display license plates, and every Texas license plate is issued by the State. Texas also owns the designs on its license plates, including the designs that Texas adopts on the basis of proposals made by private individuals and organizations. And Texas dictates the manner in which drivers may dispose of unused plates.

Texas license plates are, essentially, government IDs. And issuers of ID "typically do not permit" the placement on their IDs of "message[s] with which they do not wish to be associated Consequently, "persons who observe" designs on IDs "routinely—and reasonably—interpret them as conveying some message on the [issuer's] behalf." Indeed, a person who displays a message on a Texas license plate likely intends to convey to the public that the State has endorsed that message. If not, the individual could simply display the message in question in larger letters on a bumper sticker right next to the plate. But the individual prefers a license plate design to the purely private speech expressed through bumper stickers. That may well be because Texas's license plate designs convey government agreement with the message displayed.

[Texas] maintains direct control over the messages conveyed on its specialty plates. Texas law provides that the State "has sole control over the design, typeface, color, and alphanumeric pattern for all license plates." The Board must approve every specialty plate design proposal before the design can appear on a Texas plate. And the Board and its predecessor have actively exercised this authority. Texas asserts, and SCV concedes, that the State has rejected at least a dozen proposed designs. Accordingly, like the city government in *Summum,* Texas "has 'effectively controlled' the messages [conveyed] by exercising 'final approval authority' over their selection."

This final approval authority allows Texas to choose how to present itself and its constituency. Thus, Texas offers plates celebrating the many educational institutions attended by its citizens. But it need not issue plates deriding schooling. Texas offers plates that pay tribute to the Texas citrus industry. But it need not issue plates praising Florida's oranges as far better. And Texas offers plates that say "Fight Terrorism." But it need not issue plates promoting al Qaeda.

These considerations, taken together, convince us that the specialty plates here in question are similar enough to the monuments in *Summum* to call for the same result. That is not to say that every element of our discussion in *Summum* is relevant here. For instance, in *Summum* we emphasized that monuments were "permanent" and we observed that "public parks can accommodate only a limited number of permanent monuments." [Here,] a State could theoretically offer a much larger number of license plate designs, and those designs need not be available for time immemorial.

But those characteristics of the speech at issue in *Summum* were particularly important because the government speech at issue occurred in public parks, which are traditional public forums for "the delivery of speeches and the holding of marches and demonstrations" by private citizens. By contrast, license plates are not traditional public forums for private speech. * * *

C. SCV believes that Texas's specialty license plate designs are not government speech, at least with respect to the designs [proposed] by private parties. According to SCV, the State does not engage in expressive activity through such slogans and graphics, but rather provides a forum for private speech by making license plates available to display the private parties' designs. We cannot agree.

We have previously used what we have called "forum analysis" to evaluate government restrictions on purely private speech that occurs on government property. But [because] the State is speaking on its own behalf, the First Amendment strictures that attend the various types of government-established forums do not apply.

The parties agree that Texas's specialty license plates are not a "traditional public forum," such as a street or a park. ["The] Court has rejected the view that traditional public forum status extends beyond its historic confines." And state-issued specialty license plates lie far beyond those confines.

It is equally clear that Texas's specialty plates are neither a "'designated public forum,'" which exists where "government property that has not traditionally been regarded as a public forum is intentionally opened up for that purpose," nor a "limited public forum," which exists where a government has "reserv[ed a forum] for certain groups or for the discussion of certain topics." [Rosenberger]. A government "does not create a public forum by inaction or by permitting limited discourse, but only by intentionally opening a nontraditional forum for public discourse." * * *

Texas's policies and the nature of its license plates indicate that the State did not intend its specialty license plates to serve as either a designated public forum or a limited public forum. First, the State exercises final authority over each specialty license plate design. [Second,] Texas takes ownership of each specialty plate design, making it particularly untenable that the State intended specialty plates to serve as a forum for public discourse. Finally, Texas license plates have traditionally been used for government speech, are primarily used as a form of government ID, and bear the State's name. These features of Texas license plates indicate that Texas explicitly associates itself with the speech on its plates.

For similar reasons, we conclude that Texas's specialty license plates are not a "nonpublic for[um]," which exists "[w]here the government is acting as a proprietor, managing its internal operations." With respect to specialty license plate designs, Texas is not simply managing government property, but instead is engaging in expressive conduct. * * *

The fact that private parties take part in the design and propagation of a message does not extinguish the governmental nature of the message or transform the government's role into that of a mere forum-provider. [In] this case, as in *Summum,* the "government entity may exercise [its] freedom to express its views" even "when it receives assistance from private sources for the purpose of delivering a government-controlled message."
* * *

Of course, Texas allows many more license plate designs than the city in *Summum* allowed monuments. But our holding in *Summum* was not dependent on the precise number of monuments found within the park. Indeed, we indicated that the permanent displays in New York City's Central Park also constitute government speech. Further, there may well be many more messages that Texas wishes to convey through its license plates than there were messages that the city in *Summum* wished to convey through its monuments. Texas's desire to communicate numerous messages does not mean that the messages conveyed are not Texas's own.
* * *

IV. Our determination that Texas's specialty license plate designs are government speech does not mean that the designs do not also implicate the free speech rights of private persons. We have acknowledged that drivers who display a State's selected license plate designs convey the messages communicated through those designs. Wooley v. Maynard. And we have recognized that the First Amendment stringently limits a State's authority to compel a private party to express a view with which the private party disagrees. But here, compelled private speech is not at issue. And just as Texas cannot require SCV to convey "the State's ideological message," [Wooley], SCV cannot force Texas to include a Confederate battle flag on its specialty license plates. * * *

[Reversed].

JUSTICE ALITO, with whom THE CHIEF JUSTICE, JUSTICE SCALIA, and JUSTICE KENNEDY join, dissenting.

The Court's decision passes off private speech as government speech and, in doing so, establishes a precedent that threatens private speech that government finds displeasing. Under our First Amendment cases, the distinction between government speech and private speech is critical. The First Amendment "does not regulate government speech," and therefore when government speaks, it is free "to select the views that it wants to express." By contrast, "[i]n the realm of private speech or expression, government regulation may not favor one speaker over another."

Unfortunately, the Court's decision categorizes private speech as government speech and thus strips it of all First Amendment protection. The Court holds that all the privately created messages on the many specialty plates issued by the State of Texas convey a government message rather than the message of the motorist displaying the plate. Can this possibly be correct?

Here is a test. Suppose you sat by the side of a Texas highway and studied the license plates on the vehicles passing by. You would see, in addition to the standard Texas plates, an impressive array of specialty plates. (There are now more than 350 varieties.) You would likely observe plates that honor numerous colleges and universities. You might see plates bearing the name of a high school, a fraternity or sorority, the Masons, the Knights of Columbus, the Daughters of the American Revolution, a realty company, a favorite soft drink, a favorite burger restaurant, and a favorite NASCAR driver.

As you sat there watching these plates speed by, would you really think that the sentiments reflected in these specialty plates are the views of the State of Texas and not those of the owners of the cars? If a car with a plate that says "Rather Be Golfing" passed by at 8:30 am on a Monday morning, would you think: "This is the official policy of the State—better to golf than to work?" If you did your viewing at the start of the college football season and you saw Texas plates with the names of the University of Texas's out-of-state competitors in upcoming games—Notre Dame, Oklahoma State, the University of Oklahoma, Kansas State, Iowa State— would you assume that the State of Texas was officially (and perhaps treasonously) rooting for the Longhorns' opponents? And when a car zipped by with a plate that reads "NASCAR—24 Jeff Gordon," would you think that Gordon (born in California, raised in Indiana, resides in North Carolina) is the official favorite of the State government?

The Court says that all of these messages are government speech. It is essential that government be able to express its own viewpoint, the Court reminds us, because otherwise, how would it promote its programs, like recycling and vaccinations? So when Texas issues a "Rather Be Golfing" plate, but not a "Rather Be Playing Tennis" or "Rather Be Bowling" plate, it is furthering a state policy to promote golf but not tennis or bowling. And when Texas allows motorists to obtain a Notre Dame license plate but not a University of Southern California plate, it is taking sides in that long-time rivalry.

This capacious understanding of government speech takes a large and painful bite out of the First Amendment. Specialty plates may seem innocuous. [But] the precedent this case sets is dangerous. While all license plates unquestionably contain *some* government speech (e.g., the name of the State and the numbers and/or letters identifying the vehicle), the State of Texas has converted the remaining space on its specialty plates into little mobile billboards on which motorists can display their own messages. And what Texas did here was to reject one of the messages that members of a private group wanted to post on some of these little billboards because the

State thought that many of its citizens would find the message offensive. That is blatant viewpoint discrimination.

If the State can do this with its little mobile billboards, could it do the same with big, stationary billboards? Suppose that a State erected electronic billboards along its highways. Suppose that the State posted some government messages on these billboards and then, to raise money, allowed private entities and individuals to purchase the right to post their own messages. And suppose that the State allowed only those messages that it liked or found not too controversial. Would that be constitutional?

What if a state college or university did the same thing with a similar billboard or a campus bulletin board or dorm list serve? What if it allowed private messages that are consistent with prevailing views on campus but banned those that disturbed some students or faculty? Can there be any doubt that these examples of viewpoint discrimination would violate the First Amendment? I hope not, but the future uses of today's precedent remain to be seen.

I.   A. Specialty plates like those involved in this case are a recent development. [Once] the idea of specialty plates took hold, the number of varieties quickly multiplied, and today [Texas] motorists can choose from more than 350 messages, including many designs proposed by nonprofit groups or by individuals and for-profit businesses through the State's third-party vendor. Drivers can select plates advertising organizations and causes like 4-H, the Boy Scouts, the American Legion, Be a Blood Donor, the Girl Scouts, Insure Texas Kids, Mothers Against Drunk Driving, Marine Mammal Recovery, Save Texas Ocelots, Share the Road, Texas Reads, Texas Realtors ("I am a Texas Realtor"), the Texas State Rifle Association ("WWW.TSRA.COM"), the Texas Trophy Hunters Association, the World Wildlife Fund, the YMCA, and Young Lawyers. There are plates for fraternities and sororities and for in-state schools, both public (like Texas A & M and Texas Tech) and private (like Trinity University and Baylor). An even larger number of schools from out-of-state are honored: Arizona State, Brigham Young, Florida State, Michigan State, Alabama, and South Carolina, to name only a few. There are political slogans, like "Come and Take It" and "Don't Tread on Me," and plates promoting the citrus industry and the "Cotton Boll." Commercial businesses can have specialty plates, too. There are plates advertising Remax ("Get It Sold with Remax"), Dr. Pepper ("Always One of a Kind"), and Mighty Fine Burgers.

B.   The Texas Division of Sons of Confederate Veterans (SCV) is an organization composed of descendants of Confederate soldiers. The group applied for a Texas specialty license plate in 2009 and again in 2010. Their proposed design featured a controversial symbol, the Confederate battle flag, surrounded by the words "Sons of Confederate Veterans 1896" and a gold border. The Texas Department of Motor Vehicles Board (or Board) invited public comments and considered the plate design at a meeting in April 2011. [The] Board then voted unanimously against approval. * * *

[At] the same meeting, the Board approved a Buffalo Soldiers plate design by a 5-to-3 vote. Proceeds from fees paid by motorists who select that plate benefit the Buffalo Soldier National Museum in Houston, which is "dedicated primarily to preserving the legacy and honor of the African American soldier." "Buffalo Soldiers" is a nickname that was originally given to black soldiers in the Army's 10th Cavalry Regiment, which was formed after the Civil War, and the name was later used to describe other black soldiers. The original Buffalo Soldiers fought with distinction in the Indian Wars, but the "Buffalo Soldiers" plate was opposed by some Native Americans. One leader commented that he felt " 'the same way about the Buffalo Soldiers' " as African-Americans felt about the Confederate flag. * * *

II.   A. In relying almost entirely on one precedent—*Summum*—the Court holds that messages that private groups succeed in placing on Texas license plates are government messages. The Court badly misunderstands *Summum*. In *Summum,* a private group claimed the right to erect a large stone monument in a small city park. The 2.5-acre park contained 15 permanent displays, 11 of which had been donated by private parties. The central question concerned the nature of the municipal government's conduct when it accepted privately donated monuments for placement in its park: Had the city created a forum for private speech, or had it accepted donated monuments that expressed a government message? We held that the monuments represented government speech, and we identified several important factors that led to this conclusion.

First, governments have long used monuments as a means of expressing a government message. As we put it, "[s]ince ancient times, kings, emperors, and other rulers have erected statues of themselves to remind their subjects of their authority and power." [Thus,] long experience has led the public to associate public monuments with government speech.

Second, there is no history of landowners allowing their property to be used by third parties as the site of large permanent monuments that do not express messages that the landowners wish to convey. While "[a] great many of the monuments that adorn the Nation's public parks were financed with private funds or donated by private parties," "cities and other jurisdictions take some care in accepting donated monuments" and select those that "conve[y] a government message." We were not presented in *Summum* with any examples of public parks that had been thrown open for private groups or individuals to put up whatever monuments they desired.

Third, spatial limitations played a prominent part in our analysis. "[P]ublic parks can accommodate only a limited number of permanent monuments," and consequently permanent monuments "monopolize the use of the land on which they stand and interfere permanently with other uses of public space." Because only a limited number of monuments can be built in any given space, governments do not allow their parks to be cluttered with monuments that do not serve a government purpose, a point well understood by those who visit parks and view the monuments they contain.

These characteristics, which rendered public monuments government speech in *Summum,* are not present in Texas's specialty plate program.

B.   1. [As] we said in *Summum,* governments have used monuments since time immemorial to express important government messages, and there is no history of governments giving equal space to those wishing to express dissenting views. In 1775, when a large gilded equestrian statue of King George III dominated Bowling Green, a small park in lower Manhattan, the colonial governor surely would not have permitted the construction on that land of a monument to the fallen at Lexington and Concord. When the United States accepted the Third French Republic's gift of the Statue of Liberty in 1877, Congress, it seems safe to say, would not have welcomed a gift of a Statue of Authoritarianism if one had been offered by another country. Nor is it likely that the National Park Service today would be receptive if private groups, pointing to the Lincoln Memorial, the Martin Luther King, Jr., Memorial, and the Vietnam Veterans Memorial on the National Mall, sought permission to put up monuments to Jefferson Davis, Orval Faubus, or the North Vietnamese Army. Governments have always used public monuments to express a government message, and members of the public understand this.

The history of messages on license plates is quite different. After the beginning of motor vehicle registration in 1917, more than 70 years passed before the proliferation of specialty plates in Texas. It was not until the 1990's that motorists were allowed to choose from among 10 messages, such as "Read to Succeed" and "Keep Texas Beautiful." Up to this point, the words on the Texas plates can be considered government speech. The messages were created by the State, and they plausibly promoted state programs. But when, at some point within the last 20 years or so, the State began to allow private entities to secure plates conveying their own messages, Texas crossed the line.

[In] an attempt to gather historical support for its position, the Court relies on plates with the mottos or symbols of other States. [But] this history is irrelevant for present purposes. Like the 1991 Texas plate, these [plates] were created by the States that issued them, and motorists generally had no choice but to accept them. The words and symbols on plates of this sort were and are government speech, but plates that are essentially commissioned by private entities (at a cost that exceeds $8,000) and that express a message chosen by those entities are very different—and quite new. * * *

2.   The Texas specialty plate program also does not exhibit the "selective receptivity" present in *Summum*. To the contrary, Texas's program is *not* selective by design. The Board's chairman, who is charged with approving designs, explained that the program's purpose is "to encourage private plates" in order to "generate additional revenue for the state." And most of the time, the Board "base[s] [its] decisions on rules that primarily deal with reflectivity and readability." A Department brochure explains: "Q. Who provides the plate design? A. You do, though your design is subject to reflectivity, legibility, and design standards."

Pressed to come up with any evidence that the State has exercised "selective receptivity," Texas (and the Court) rely primarily on sketchy information not contained in the record, specifically that the Board's predecessor (might have) rejected a "pro-life" plate and perhaps others on the ground that they contained messages that were offensive. But even if this happened, it shows only that the present case may not be the only one in which the State has exercised viewpoint discrimination.

Texas's only other (also extrarecord) evidence of selectivity concerns a proposed plate that was thought to create a threat to the fair enforcement of the State's motor vehicle laws. This proposed plate was a Texas DPS Troopers Foundation (Troopers) plate, proposed in 2012. The Board considered that proposed plate at an August 2012 meeting, at which it approved six other plate designs without discussion, but it rejected the Troopers plate in a deadlocked vote due to apparent concern that the plate could give the impression that those displaying it would receive favored treatment from state troopers. The constitutionality of this Board action does not necessarily turn on whether approval of this plate would have made the message government speech. If, as I believe, the Texas specialty plate program created a limited public forum, private speech may be excluded if it is inconsistent with the purpose of the forum.

Thus, even if Texas's extrarecord information is taken into account, the picture here is different from that in *Summum*. Texas does not take care to approve only those proposed plates that convey messages that the State supports. Instead, it proclaims that it is open to all private messages—except those, like the SCV plate, that would offend some who viewed them.

The Court believes that messages on privately created plates are government speech because motorists want a seal of state approval for their messages and therefore prefer plates over bumper stickers. This is dangerous reasoning. There is a big difference between government speech (that is, speech by the government in furtherance of its programs) and governmental blessing (or condemnation) of private speech. Many private speakers in a forum would welcome a sign of government approval. But in the realm of private speech, government regulation may not favor one viewpoint over another.

3. A final factor that was important in *Summum* was space. A park can accommodate only so many permanent monuments. Often large and made of stone, monuments can last for centuries and are difficult to move. License plates, on the other hand, are small, light, mobile, and designed to last for only a relatively brief time. The only absolute limit on the number of specialty plates that a State could issue is the number of registered vehicles. The variety of available plates is limitless, too. Today Texas offers more than 350 varieties. In 10 years, might it be 3,500?

In sum, the Texas specialty plate program has none of the factors that were critical in *Summum,* and the Texas program exhibits a very important characteristic that was missing in that case: Individuals who want to display a Texas specialty plate, instead of the standard plate, must pay an increased annual registration fee. How many groups or individuals would clamor to pay $8,000 (the cost of the deposit required to create a new plate) in order to broadcast the government's message as opposed to their own? And if Texas really wants to speak out in support of, say, Iowa State University (but not the University of Iowa) or "Young Lawyers" (but not old ones), why must it be paid to say things that it really wants to say? The fees Texas collects pay for much more than merely the administration of the program. States have not adopted specialty license plate programs like Texas's because they are now bursting with things they want to say on their license plates. Those programs were adopted because they bring in money. [Texas] has space available on millions of little mobile billboards. And Texas, in effect, sells that space to those who wish to use it to express a personal message—provided only that the message does not express a viewpoint that the State finds unacceptable. That is not government speech; it is the regulation of private speech.

III. What Texas has done by selling space on its license plates is to create what we have called a limited public forum. It has allowed state property [to] be used by private speakers according to rules that the State prescribes. Under the First Amendment, however, those rules cannot discriminate on the basis of viewpoint. But that is exactly what Texas did here. The Board rejected Texas SCV's design, "specifically the confederate flag portion of the design, because public comments have shown that many members of the general public find the design offensive, and because such comments are reasonable." These statements indisputably demonstrate that the Board denied Texas SCV's design because of its viewpoint.

The Confederate battle flag is a controversial symbol. To the Texas Sons of Confederate Veterans, it is said to evoke the memory of their ancestors and other soldiers who fought for the South in the Civil War. To others, it symbolizes slavery, segregation, and hatred. Whatever it means to motorists who display that symbol and to those who see it, the flag expresses a viewpoint. The Board rejected the plate design because it concluded that many Texans would find the flag symbol offensive. That was pure viewpoint discrimination.

If the Board's candid explanation of its reason for rejecting the SCV plate were not alone sufficient to establish this point, the Board's approval of the Buffalo Soldiers plate at the same meeting dispels any doubt. The proponents of both the SCV and Buffalo Soldiers plates saw them as honoring soldiers who served with bravery and honor in the past. To the opponents of both plates, the images on the plates evoked painful memories. The Board rejected one plate and approved the other.

Like these two plates, many other specialty plates have the potential to irritate and perhaps even infuriate those who see them. Texas allows a plate with the words "Choose Life," but the State of New York rejected such a plate because the message "[is] so incredibly divisive." Texas allows a specialty plate honoring the Boy Scouts, but the group's refusal to accept gay leaders angers some. Virginia, another State with a proliferation of specialty plates, issues plates for controversial organizations like the National Rifle Association, controversial commercial enterprises (raising tobacco and mining coal), controversial sports (fox hunting), and a professional sports team with a controversial name (the Washington Redskins). Allowing States to reject specialty plates based on their potential to offend is viewpoint discrimination.

The Board's decision cannot be saved by its suggestion that the plate, if allowed, "could distract or disturb some drivers to the point of being unreasonably dangerous." This rationale cannot withstand strict scrutiny. Other States allow specialty plates with the Confederate Battle Flag, and Texas has not pointed to evidence that these plates have led to incidents of road rage or accidents. Texas does not ban bumper stickers bearing the image of the Confederate battle flag. Nor does it ban any of the many other bumper stickers that convey political messages and other messages that are capable of exciting the ire of those who loathe the ideas they express.

[* * * I] respectfully dissent.

III. GOVERNMENT AS EMPLOYER

P. 1088, at end of fn. 303:

See also *Heffernan v. City of Paterson, N.J.* (above, Supp. to Ch. 7, Sec. 2, at p. 850).

9. THE RIGHT NOT TO SPEAK, THE RIGHT TO ASSOCIATE, AND THE RIGHT NOT TO ASSOCIATE

I. THE RIGHT NOT TO BE ASSOCIATED WITH PARTICULAR IDEAS

P. 1153, add fn. 357a at end of first paragraph of note 8:

[357a] In its 2015 Term, the Court granted certiorari in *Friedrichs v. California Teachers Ass'n*, 2013 WL 9825479 (C.D. Cal., Dec. 5, 2013), aff'd, 2014 WL 10076847 (9th Cir., Nov. 18. 2014), and the case was briefed, argued, and widely understood to be a reconsideration of *Abood*'s holding that non-members of a public employee union can still be required to pay for the union's collective bargaining expenses, even if not for the union's political expenses. After briefing, argument, and Justice Scalia's death, however, the decision below (relying on *Abood*) was affirmed without opinion by an equally divided court, 136 S.Ct. 1083 (2016).

10. WEALTH AND THE POLITICAL PROCESS: CONCERNS FOR EQUALITY

P. 1205, at end:

8. ***Judicial elections.*** In most but not all American states, judges are elected. When judges are running for election or re-election, do the principles of *Buckley v. Valeo, Citizens United*, and most of the other campaign finance cases discussed above apply in the same way that they apply to legislative and executive elections? In WILLIAMS-YULEE v. FLORIDA BAR, 135 S.Ct. 1656 (2015), a sharply and intricately divided 5–4 Court, per ROBERTS, C.J., on most of the issues, said "no," concluding that concerns with judicial integrity upheld restrictions on solicitation of campaign funds by judges, restrictions that would have been invalidated on First Amendment grounds with respect to candidates for non-judicial offices.

CHAPTER 8

FREEDOM OF RELIGION

■ ■ ■

2. FREE EXERCISE CLAUSE AND RELATED PROBLEMS

I. CONFLICT WITH STATE REGULATION

P. 1305, after note 2(e):

(f)   In TRINITY LUTHERAN CHURCH of COLUMBUS, Inc. v. COMER, 137 S.Ct. 2012 (2017), Missouri refused to reimburse a church for the cost of gravel produced by the state pursuant to its program to dispose of scrapped tires. The church wished to use the gravel to resurface its school's playground. The state relied on a provision of the state constitution forbidding aid to churches. The Court, per ROBERTS, C.J., held that this violated the Free Exercise Clause: The state's "policy expressly discriminates against otherwise eligible recipients." Consequently, it "imposes a penalty on the free exercise of religion that triggers the most exacting scrutiny, *Lukumi*." *Locke* is distinguishable because its use of tax funds to pay for training of clergy involved an "essentially religious endeavor," totally unlike Missouri's program to use recycled tires to resurface playgrounds.

Thomas, J., joined by Gorsuch J., concurred in part. Gorsuch, J., joined by Thomas, J. also concurred in part. Breyer, J., concurred in the result and would limit it to the fact that the program here was "designed to secure or to improve the health and safety of children."

SOTOMAYOR, J., joined by Ginsburg, J. dissented: The Court holds "for the first time, that the Constitution requires the government to provide public funds directly to a church. [The] Establishment Clause does not allow Missouri to grant the Church's funding requests because the Church uses the Learning Center, including its playground, in conjunction with its religious mission. The Court's silence on this front signals its misunderstanding of the facts of this case or a departure from our precedents."

Are you persuaded by the plurality's suggestion in a footnote that playground resurfacing differs from other contexts in which religious discrimination may occur?

CHAPTER 9

EQUAL PROTECTION

■ ■ ■

2. RACE AND ETHNIC ANCESTRY

V. AFFIRMATIVE ACTION

A. Affirmative Action in Higher Education

P. 1439, substitute for *Grutter v. Bollinger*, *Gratz v. Bollinger*, *Fisher v. University of Texas*, and all of the Notes and Questions that follow those cases on pages 1439–1462:

GRUTTER V. BOLLINGER
539 U.S. 306, 123 S.Ct. 2325, 156 L.Ed.2d 304 (2003).

JUSTICE O'CONNOR delivered the opinion of the Court.

This case requires us to decide whether the use of race as a factor in student admissions by the University of Michigan Law School (Law School) is unlawful.

I A. The Law School ranks among the Nation's top law schools. It receives more than 3,500 applications each year for a class of around 350 students. The hallmark of [the Law School's admission] policy is its focus on academic ability coupled with a flexible assessment of applicants' talents, experiences, and potential "to contribute to the learning of those around them." [In] reviewing an applicant's file, admissions officials must consider the applicant's undergraduate grade point average (GPA) and Law School Admissions Test (LSAT) score because they are important (if imperfect) predictors of academic success in law school. [But] so-called "soft variables" such as "the enthusiasm of recommenders, the quality of the undergraduate institution, the quality of the applicant's essay, and the areas and difficulty of undergraduate course selection" are all brought to bear in assessing an "applicant's likely contributions to the intellectual and social life of the institution."

[The] policy aspires to "achieve that diversity which has the potential to enrich everyone's education and thus make a law school class stronger than the sum of its parts." [By] enrolling a "critical mass of [underrepresented] minority students," the Law School seeks to "ensur[e] their ability to make unique contributions to the character of the Law School."

B.   Petitioner Barbara Grutter is a white Michigan resident who applied to the Law School in 1996 with a 3.8 grade point average and 161 LSAT score. The Law School initially placed petitioner on a waiting list, but subsequently rejected her application. [She then filed suit alleging that University officials] discriminated against her on the basis of race in violation of the Fourteenth Amendment [and civil rights statutes including the 1964 Civil Rights Act].

[During] the 15-day bench trial, the parties introduced extensive evidence concerning the Law School's use of race in the admissions process. [A former admissions director] testified that at the height of the admissions season, he would frequently consult the so-called "daily reports" that kept track of the racial and ethnic composition of the class (along with other information such as residency status and gender). This was done, [he] testified, to ensure that a critical mass of underrepresented minority students would be reached so as to realize the educational benefits of a diverse student body. [An expert witness testified] that in 2000, [underrepresented] minority students would have comprised 4 percent of the entering class in 2000 instead of the actual figure of 14.5 percent. * * *

II.   We last addressed the use of race in public higher education over 25 years ago [in] the landmark *Bakke* case. [Justice] Powell approved the university's use of race to further only one interest: "the attainment of a diverse student body." * * * [We] apply strict scrutiny to all racial classifications to " 'smoke out' illegitimate uses of race by assuring that [government] is pursuing a goal important enough to warrant use of a highly suspect tool." *Richmond v. J.A. Croson Co.* Strict scrutiny is not "strict in theory, but fatal in fact." *Adarand Constructors, Inc. v. Pena*, 515 U.S. 200 (1995). [When] race-based action is necessary to further a compelling governmental interest, such action does not violate the constitutional guarantee of equal protection so long as the narrow-tailoring requirement is also satisfied.

III A.   [Although] some language in [past] opinions might be read to suggest that remedying past discrimination is the only permissible justification for race-based governmental action[, we]have never held that the only governmental use of race that can survive strict scrutiny is remedying past discrimination. [The] Law School has a compelling interest in attaining a diverse student body. The Law School's educational judgment that such diversity is essential to its educational mission is one to which we defer. * * *

As part of its goal of "assembling a class that is both exceptionally academically qualified and broadly diverse," the Law School seeks to "enroll a 'critical mass' of minority students." The Law School's interest is not simply "to assure within its student body some specified percentage of a particular group merely because of its race or ethnic origin." That would amount to outright racial balancing, which is patently unconstitutional. Rather, the Law School's concept of critical mass is defined by reference to the educational benefits that diversity is designed to produce. These benefits are substantial. As the District Court emphasized, the Law School's admissions policy promotes "cross-racial understanding," helps to break down racial stereotypes, and "enables [students] to better understand persons of different races." [Major] American businesses have made clear that the skills needed in today's increasingly global marketplace can only be developed through exposure to widely diverse people, cultures, ideas, and viewpoints. What is more, high-ranking retired officers and civilian leaders of the United States military assert that, "[b]ased on [their] decades of experience," a "highly qualified, racially diverse officer corps is essential to the military's ability to fulfill its principle mission to provide national security." The primary sources for the Nation's officer corps are the service academies and the Reserve Officers Training Corps (ROTC), the latter comprising students already admitted to participating colleges and universities. At present, "the military cannot achieve an officer corps that is *both* highly qualified *and* racially diverse unless the service academies and the ROTC used limited race-conscious recruiting and admissions policies." To fulfill its mission, the military "must be selective in admissions for training and education for the officer corps, and it must train and educate a highly qualified, racially diverse officer corps in a racially diverse setting." Ibid. We agree that "[i]t requires only a small step from this analysis to conclude that our country's other most selective institutions must remain both diverse and selective."

[U]niversities, and in particular, law schools, represent the training ground for a large number of our Nation's leaders. *Sweatt v. Painter.* [In] order to cultivate a set of leaders with legitimacy in the eyes of the citizenry, it is necessary that the path to leadership be visibly open to talented and qualified individuals of every race and ethnicity. All members of our heterogeneous society must have confidence in the openness and integrity of the educational institutions that provide this training. * * *

B. Even in the limited circumstance when drawing racial distinctions is permissible to further a compelling state interest, government is still "constrained in how it may pursue that end." [A] university may consider race or ethnicity only as a " 'plus' in a particular applicant's file," without "insulat[ing] the individual from comparison with all other candidates for the available seats." [We] find that the Law School's admissions program bears the hallmarks of a narrowly tailored plan. [The] Law School's goal of attaining a critical mass of underrepresented minority students does not transform its program into a quota. [Nor] does the Law School's consultation of the "daily reports," which keep track of the racial and ethnic composition of the class (as well as of residency and gender), "sugges[t] there was no further attempt at individual review save for race itself" during the final stages of the admissions process. To the contrary, the Law School's admissions officers testified without contradiction that they never gave race any more or less weight based on the information contained in these reports. Moreover, [between] 1993 and 1998, the number of African-American, Latino, and Native-American students in each class at the Law School varied from 13.5 to 20.1 percent, a range inconsistent with a quota.

[Petitioner] and the United States argue that the Law School's plan is not narrowly tailored because race-neutral means exist to obtain the educational benefits of student body diversity that the Law School seeks. We disagree. Narrow tailoring does not require exhaustion of every conceivable race-neutral alternative. Nor does it require a university to choose between maintaining a reputation for excellence or fulfilling a commitment to provide educational opportunities to members of all racial groups. [The] District Court took the Law School to task for failing to consider race-neutral alternatives such as "using a lottery system" or "decreasing the emphasis for all applicants on undergraduate GPA and LSAT scores." But these alternatives would require a dramatic sacrifice of diversity, the academic quality of all admitted students, or both. [The] United States advocates "percentage plans," recently adopted by public undergraduate institutions in Texas, Florida, and California to guarantee admission to all students above a certain class-rank threshold in every high school in the State. [In part because some high schools have disproportionately large minority enrollments, these programs help to increase minority admissions, though often less so than explicitly race-based affirmative action programs.] The United States does not, however, explain how such plans could work for graduate and professional schools.

[We] acknowledge that "there are serious problems of justice connected with the idea of preference itself." [It] has been 25 years since Justice Powell first approved the use of race to further an interest in student body diversity in the context of public higher education. Since that time, the number of minority applicants with high grades and test scores has indeed increased. We expect that 25 years from now, the use of racial preferences will no longer be necessary to further the interest approved today.

JUSTICE GINSBURG, with whom JUSTICE BREYER joins, concurring.

[From] today's vantage point, one may hope, but not firmly forecast, that over the next generation's span, progress toward nondiscrimination and genuinely equal opportunity will make it safe to sunset affirmative action.

CHIEF JUSTICE REHNQUIST, with whom JUSTICE SCALIA, JUSTICE KENNEDY, and JUSTICE THOMAS join, dissenting.

I agree with the Court that, "in the limited circumstance when drawing racial distinctions is permissible," the government must ensure that its means are narrowly tailored to achieve a compelling state interest. I do not believe, however, that the University of Michigan Law School's (Law School) means are narrowly tailored to the interest it asserts. [Stripped] of its "critical mass" veil, the Law School's program is revealed as a naked effort to achieve racial balancing.

[From] 1995 through 2000, the Law School admitted between 1,130 and 1,310 students. Of those, between 13 and 19 were Native American, between 91 and 108 were African-Americans, and between 47 and 56 were Hispanic. If the Law School is admitting between 91 and 108 African-Americans in order to achieve "critical mass," thereby preventing African-American students from feeling "isolated or like spokespersons for their race," one would think that a number of the same order of magnitude would be necessary to accomplish the same purpose for Hispanics and Native Americans. Similarly, even if all of the Native American applicants admitted in a given year matriculate, which the record demonstrates is not at all the case,* how can this possibly constitute a "critical mass" of Native Americans in a class of over 350 students? * * *

These different numbers, moreover, come only as a result of substantially different treatment among the three underrepresented minority groups. [For] example, in 2000, 12 Hispanics who scored between a 159–160 on the LSAT and earned a GPA of 3.00 or higher applied for admission and only 2 were admitted. Meanwhile, 12 African-Americans in the same range of qualifications applied for admission and all 12 were admitted. Likewise, that same year, 16 Hispanics who scored between a 151–153 on the LSAT and earned a 3.00 or higher applied for admission and only 1 of those applicants was admitted. Twenty-three similarly qualified African-Americans applied for admission and 14 were admitted.

Only when the "critical mass" label is discarded does a likely explanation for these numbers emerge. [The] correlation between the percentage of the Law School's pool of applicants who are members of the three minority groups and the percentage of the admitted applicants who are members of these same groups is far too precise to be dismissed as merely the result of the school paying "some attention to [the] numbers." As the tables below show, from 1995 through 2000 the percentage of admitted applicants who were members of these minority groups closely tracked the percentage of individuals in the school's applicant pool who were from the same groups.

---

* **[Ct's Note]** Indeed, during this 5-year time period, enrollment of Native American students dropped to as low as three such students. Any assertion that such a small group constituted a "critical mass" of Native Americans is simply absurd.

For example, in 1995, when 9.7% of the applicant pool was African-American, 9.4% of the admitted class was African-American. By 2000, only 7.5% of the applicant pool was African-American, and 7.3% of the admitted class was African-American. [The] tight correlation between the percentage of applicants and admittees of a given race, therefore, must result from careful race based planning by the Law School. It suggests a formula for admission based on the aspirational assumption that all applicants are equally qualified academically, and therefore that the proportion of each group admitted should be the same as the proportion of that group in the applicant pool. [This] is precisely the type of racial balancing that the Court itself calls "patently unconstitutional."

JUSTICE KENNEDY, dissenting.

The opinion by Justice Powell in *Bakke*, in my view, states the correct rule for resolving this case. The Court, however, does not apply strict scrutiny. By trying to say otherwise, it undermines both the test and its own controlling precedents. [At] the very least, the constancy of admitted minority students and the close correlation between the racial breakdown of admitted minorities and the composition of the applicant pool, [require] the Law School either to produce a convincing explanation or to show it has taken adequate steps to ensure individual assessment. The Law School does neither. * * *

JUSTICE SCALIA, with whom JUSTICE THOMAS joins, concurring in part and dissenting in part.

The "educational benefit" that the University of Michigan seeks to achieve by racial discrimination consists, according to the Court, of "cross-racial understanding," and "better prepar[ation of] students for an increasingly diverse workforce and society," all of which is necessary not only for work, but also for good "citizenship." This is not, of course, an "educational benefit" on which students will be graded on their Law School transcript (Works and Plays Well with Others: B+) or tested by the bar examiners (Q: Describe in 500 words or less your cross-racial understanding). For it is a lesson of life rather than law—essentially the same lesson taught to (or rather learned by, for it cannot be "taught" in the usual sense) people three feet shorter and twenty years younger than the full-grown adults at the University of Michigan Law School, in institutions ranging from Boy Scout troops to public-school kindergartens. If properly considered an "educational benefit" at all, it is surely not one that is either uniquely relevant to law school or uniquely "teachable" in a formal educational setting. *And therefore*: If it is appropriate for the University of Michigan Law School to use racial discrimination for the purpose of putting together a "critical mass" that will convey generic lessons in socialization and good citizenship, surely it is no less appropriate—indeed, *particularly* appropriate—for the civil service system of the State of Michigan to do so.

There, also, those exposed to "critical masses" of certain races will presumably become better Americans, better Michiganders, better civil servants. And surely private employers cannot be criticized—indeed, should be praised—if they also "teach" good citizenship to their adult employees through a patriotic, all-American system of racial discrimination in hiring. The nonminority individuals who are deprived of a legal education, a civil service job, or any job at all by reason of their skin color will surely understand.

Unlike a clear constitutional holding that racial preferences in state educational institutions are impermissible, or even a clear anticonstitutional holding that racial preferences in state educational institutions are OK, today's [decision in *Grutter*, when coupled with the Court's decision in *Gratz*, which follows immediately,] seems perversely designed to prolong the controversy and the litigation. Some future lawsuits will presumably focus on whether the discriminatory scheme in question contains enough evaluation of the applicant "as an individual," and sufficiently avoids "separate admissions tracks" [to be constitutionally permissible]. Some will focus on whether a university has gone beyond the bounds of a " 'good faith effort' " and has so zealously pursued its "critical mass" as to make it an unconstitutional de facto quota system, rather than merely " 'a permissible goal.' " [Finally], litigation can be expected on behalf of minority groups intentionally short changed in the institution's composition of its generic minority "critical mass." I do not look forward to any of these cases. The Constitution proscribes government discrimination on the basis of race, and state-provided education is no exception.

JUSTICE THOMAS, with whom JUSTICE SCALIA joins as to Parts I–VII, concurring in part and dissenting in part.

Frederick Douglass, speaking to a group of abolitionists almost 140 years ago, delivered a message lost on today's majority: "[I]n regard to the colored people, there is always more that is benevolent, I perceive, than just, manifested towards us. What I ask for the negro is not benevolence, not pity, not sympathy, but simply *justice*. . . . And if the negro cannot stand on his own legs, let him fall. . . . All I ask is, give him a chance to stand on his own legs! Let him alone! [Y]our interference is doing him positive injury." [Like] Douglass, I believe blacks can achieve in every avenue of American life without the meddling of university administrators. Because I wish to see all students succeed whatever their color, I share, in some respect, the sympathies of those who sponsor the type of discrimination advanced by the University of Michigan Law School. [The] Constitution does not, however, tolerate institutional devotion to the status quo in admissions policies when such devotion ripens into racial discrimination. Nor does the Constitution countenance the unprecedented deference the Court gives to the Law School, an approach inconsistent with the very concept of "strict scrutiny."

III. [Justice] Powell's opinion in *Bakke* and the Court's decision today rest on the fundamentally flawed proposition that racial discrimination can be contextualized so that a goal, such as classroom aesthetics, can be compelling in one context but not in another. [Under] the proper standard, there is no pressing public necessity in maintaining a public law school at all and, it follows, certainly not an elite law school. Likewise, marginal improvements in legal education do not qualify as a compelling state interest. * * *

IV. [With] the adoption of different admissions methods, such as accepting all students who meet minimum qualifications, the Law School could achieve its vision of the racially aesthetic student body without the use of racial discrimination. The Law School concedes this, but the Court holds, implicitly and under the guise of narrow tailoring, that the Law School has a compelling state interest in doing what it wants to do. I cannot agree. First, under strict scrutiny, the Law School's assessment of the benefits of racial discrimination and devotion to the admissions status quo are not entitled to any sort of deference, grounded in the First Amendment or anywhere else. Second, even if its "academic selectivity" must be maintained at all costs along with racial discrimination, the Court ignores the fact that other top law schools have succeeded in meeting their aesthetic demands without racial discrimination. * * *

VI. [I] believe what lies beneath the Court's decision today are the benighted notions that one can tell when racial discrimination benefits (rather than hurts) minority groups, and that racial discrimination is necessary to remedy general societal ills. [I] must contest the notion that the Law School's discrimination benefits those admitted as a result of it. The Court spends considerable time discussing the impressive display of amicus support for the Law School in this case from all corners of society. But nowhere in any of the filings in this Court is any evidence that the purported "beneficiaries" of this racial discrimination prove themselves by performing at (or even near) the same level as those students who receive no preferences.

[The] Law School tantalizes unprepared students with the promise of a University of Michigan degree and all of the opportunities that it offers. These overmatched students take the bait, only to find that they cannot succeed in the cauldron of competition. And this mismatch crisis is not restricted to elite institutions. [While] these students may graduate with law degrees, there is no evidence that they have received a qualitatively better legal education (or become better lawyers) than if they had gone to a less "elite" law school for which they were better prepared.

[It] is uncontested that each year, the Law School admits a handful of blacks who would be admitted in the absence of racial discrimination. Who can differentiate between those who belong and those who do not? The majority of blacks are admitted to the Law School because of discrimination, and because of this policy all are tarred as undeserving. This problem of stigma does not depend on determinacy as to whether those stigmatized are actually the "beneficiaries" of racial discrimination. When blacks take positions in the highest places of government, industry, or academia, it is an open question today whether their skin color played a part in their advancement. The question itself is the stigma—because either racial discrimination did play a role, in which case the person may be deemed "otherwise unqualified," or it did not, in which case asking the question itself unfairly marks those blacks who would succeed without discrimination.[1]

————

In GRATZ v. BOLLINGER, 539 U.S. 244 (2003), the Court, per REHNQUIST, C.J., invalidated a rigid program for undergraduate admissions to the University of Michigan under which applicants from underrepresented minorities received a fixed total of 20 points out of a possible 150 on the school's admission index. The index assigned 110 points for high school grades, standardized test scores, and rigor of academic program. "Legacy" applicants whose parents had attended the school received four points. Apart from race, the index awarded 20 points to students from socioeconomically disadvantaged backgrounds, recruited athletes, and those specially designated by the provost. Focusing solely on the race-based preference, the Court assumed that the university had a compelling interest in achieving a diverse student body, but it ruled that the uniform, 20-point, race-based bonus was too large and mechanical to be narrowly tailored the kind of diversity in student background and outlook that Powell, J., had approved in *Bakke*. Breyer, J., concurred in the judgment only.

GINSBURG, J., joined by Souter, J., dissented: "The stain of generations of racial oppression is still visible in our society, and the determination to hasten its removal remains vital. One can reasonably anticipate, therefore, that colleges and universities will seek to maintain their minority enrollment—and the networks and opportunities thereby opened to minority graduates—whether or not they can do so in full candor through adoption of affirmative action plans of the kind here at issue. Without recourse to such plans, institutions of higher education may resort to camouflage. For example, schools may encourage applicants to write of

———

[1]   Compare Randall Kennedy, *For Discrimination: Race, Affirmative Action, and the Law* 124–25 (2013): "[A]ffirmative action imposes a stigmatic cost on anyone perceived to be a beneficiary. [But t]he proper response to the stigma objection is to (1) acknowledge its strength, (2) diminish avoidable harms through careful design of affirmative action programs, (3) argue against exaggerations of stigmatic harms, and (4) insist that [affirmative action's] benefits must be weighted against its drawbacks. [There] are reasons to believe that affirmative action is not so stigmatically burdensome as certain anti-affirmative action detractors suggest. Especially among racial minorities, relatively few complain about this cost, against the concomitant benefit."

their cultural traditions in the essays they submit, or to indicate whether English is their second language. Seeking to improve their chances for admission, applicants may highlight the minority group associations to which they belong, or the Hispanic surnames of their mothers or grandparents. In turn, teachers' recommendations may emphasize who a student is as much as what he or she has accomplished. If honesty is the best policy, surely Michigan's accurately described, fully disclosed College affirmative action program is preferable to achieving similar numbers through winks, nods, and disguises."

Stevens, J., also dissented.

FISHER V. UNIVERSITY OF TEXAS
___ U.S. ___, 136 S.Ct. 2198, 195 L.Ed.2d 511 (2016).

JUSTICE KENNEDY delivered the opinion of the Court.

[Abigail Fisher, a Caucasian who was denied admission to the University of Texas at Austin, brought suit challenging the University's use of race in its admissions process. The University had an unusual two-tiered admissions process. Roughly 75% of students are admitted based on their high school class rank (if they attended high school in Texas). The remaining 25% are admitted pursuant to a holistic analysis, similar but not identical to that used in *Grutter v. Bollinger*, that takes race into account. The two-tiered process had a complex history.

[Prior to 1996, the University had a race-based affirmative action program. It made its admissions decisions primarily based on an "Academic Index" (or AI), which it calculated by combining an applicant's SAT score and academic performance in high school, but gave a preference to racial minorities. The expressly race-based preferences ended temporarily in 1996, when the Court of Appeals for the Fifth Circuit held] that any consideration of race in college admissions violates the Equal Protection Clause. *See Hopwood v. Texas*, 78 F. 3d 932.

[In response,] the University [began] making admissions decisions based on an applicant's AI and his or her "Personal Achievement Index" (PAI). The PAI was a numerical score based on a holistic review [that took account of] the applicant's essays, leadership and work experience, extracurricular activities, community service, and other "special characteristics" that might give the admissions committee insight into a student's background. [Initially, however,] race was not a consideration.

[Also in response to the judicial decision banning race-based preferences, the] Texas Legislature enacted [the so-called] Top Ten Percent Law, [which guarantee admission to Texas high school students based on class rank. The] University implemented the Top Ten Percent Law in 1998 [but continued to use the combined AI and PAI assessment system to fill about 25% of the class]—again, without considering race. [Following the *Grutter* decision, however, the University conducted a study, which concluded that] its admissions policy [failed] to provide "the educational benefits of a diverse student body [to] all of the University's undergraduate students, [and established the policy that Fisher challenged.]

[Pursuant to the new policy, the University continues to use the Top Ten Percent Plan—which, by statute, can be used to fill only 75% of the class, and in fact makes admission available only to those in the top seven or eight percent of graduating seniors—to make the majority of its admissions decisions, but admits the] remaining 25 percent or so [based] on a combination of their AI and PAI scores. Now, however, race is given weight as a subfactor within the PAI.

Petitioner Abigail Fisher applied for admission to the University's 2008 freshman class. She was not in the top 10 percent of her high school class, so she was evaluated [and rejected] through holistic, full-file review. [In her complaint, she challenged the constitutionality of the holistic assessment component of the University's admissions program, but not the Top Ten Percent Plan. In the first round of litigation, the lower courts ruled against her, but the Supreme Court, in *Fisher v. University of Texas (I)*, 570 U.S. ___, 133 S.Ct. 2411 (2013), per Kennedy, J., held that the lower courts] "had applied an overly deferential "good-faith" standard in assessing the constitutionality of the University's program.

[Kennedy, J., wrote in *Fisher I*: "[Once] the University has established that its goal of diversity is consistent with strict scrutiny, [the] University must prove that [its] means are narrowly tailored to that goal. On this point, the University receives no deference. * * * Although '[n]arrow tailoring does not require exhaustion of every *conceivable* race-neutral alternative,' [strict] scrutiny imposes on the university the ultimate burden of demonstrating [that] available, workable race-neutral alternatives do not suffice." When the lower courts again rejected Fisher's challenge on the remand, the Court again granted certiorari.]

Petitioner's [failure to challenge] the Top Ten Percent Plan complicates [judicial] review [because] it has led to a record that is almost devoid of information about the students who secured admission [through] the Plan. The Court thus cannot know how students admitted solely based on their class rank differ in their contribution to diversity from students admitted through holistic review. In an ordinary case, this evidentiary gap perhaps could be filled by a remand to the district court for further fact-finding. When petitioner's application was rejected, however, the University's combined percentage-plan/holistic review approach to admission had been in effect for just three years. While studies undertaken over the eight years since then may be of significant value in determining the constitutionality of the University's current admissions policy, that evidence has little bearing on whether petitioner received equal treatment [in] 2008.

[Petitioner] long since has graduated from another college, and the University's policy—and the data on which it first was based—may have evolved or changed in material ways. The fact that this case has been litigated on a somewhat artificial basis, furthermore, may limit its value for prospective guidance.

[In] seeking to reverse the judgment of the Court of Appeals, petitioner [argues first] that the University has not articulated its compelling interest with sufficient clarity. According to petitioner, the University must set forth more precisely the level of minority enrollment that would constitute a "critical mass." As this Court's cases have made clear, however, the compelling interest that justifies consideration of race in college admissions is not an interest in enrolling a certain number of minority students. Rather, a university may institute a race-conscious admissions program as a means of obtaining "the educational benefits that flow from student body diversity." *Fisher I.* As this Court has said, enrolling a diverse student body "promotes cross-racial understanding, helps to break down racial stereotypes, and enables students to better understand persons of different races." Id. Equally important, "student body diversity promotes learning outcomes, and better prepares students for an increasingly diverse work force and society." Ibid. Increasing minority enrollment may be instrumental to these educational benefits, but it is not, as petitioner seems to suggest, a goal that can or should be reduced to pure numbers. Indeed, since the University is prohibited from seeking a particular number or quota of minority students, it cannot be faulted for failing to specify the particular level of minority enrollment at which it believes the educational benefits of diversity will be obtained. On the other hand, asserting an interest in the educational benefits of diversity writ large is insufficient. A university's goals cannot be elusory or amorphous—they must be sufficiently measurable to permit judicial scrutiny of the policies adopted to reach them.

The record reveals that in first setting forth its current admissions policy, the University articulated concrete and precise goals. On the first page of its 2004 "Proposal to Consider Race and Ethnicity in Admissions," the University identifies the educational values it seeks to realize through its admissions process: the destruction of stereotypes, the " 'promot[ion of] cross-racial understanding,' " the preparation of a student body " 'for an increasingly diverse workforce and society,' " and the " 'cultivat[ion of] a set of leaders with legitimacy in the eyes of the citizenry.' " [All] of these objectives [mirror] the "compelling interest" this Court has approved in its prior cases.

The University has provided in addition a "reasoned, principled explanation" for its decision to pursue these goals. [Before implementing the challenged policy, it conducted] a year-long study, which concluded that "[t]he use of race-neutral policies and programs ha[d] not been successful" in "provid[ing] an educational setting that fosters cross-racial understanding, provid[ing] enlightened discussion and learning, [or] prepar[ing] students to function in an increasingly diverse workforce and society." Further support for the University's conclusion can be found in the depositions and affidavits from various admissions officers, all of whom articulate the same, consistent "reasoned, principled explanation."

Second, petitioner argues that the University has no need to consider race because it had already "achieved critical mass" by 2003 using the Top Ten Percent Plan and race-neutral holistic review. Petitioner is correct that a university bears a heavy burden in showing that it had not obtained the educational benefits of diversity before it turned to a race-conscious plan. The record reveals, however, that, at the time of petitioner's application, the University could not be faulted on this score. Before changing its policy the University conducted "months of study and deliberation, including retreats, interviews, [and] review of data," and concluded that "[t]he use of race-neutral policies and programs ha[d] not been successful in achieving" sufficient racial diversity at the University. At no stage in this litigation has petitioner challenged the University's good faith in conducting its studies, and the Court properly declines to consider the extrarecord materials the dissent relies upon.

The record itself contains significant evidence, both statistical and anecdotal, in support of the University's position. To start, the demographic data the University has submitted show consistent stagnation in terms of the percentage of minority students enrolling at the University from 1996 to 2002. In 1996, for example, 266 African-American freshmen enrolled, a total that constituted 4.1 percent of the incoming class. In 2003, the year *Grutter* was decided, 267 African-American students enrolled—again, 4.1 percent of the incoming class. The numbers for Hispanic and Asian-American students tell a similar story. Although demographics alone are by no means dispositive, they do have some value as a gauge of the University's ability to enroll students who can offer underrepresented perspectives.

In addition to this broad demographic data, the University put forward evidence that minority students admitted under the *Hopwood* regime experienced feelings of loneliness and isolation.

This anecdotal evidence is, in turn, bolstered by further, more nuanced quantitative data. In 2002, 52 percent of undergraduate classes with at least five students had no African-American students enrolled in them, and

27 percent had only one African-American student. [Twelve] percent of these classes had no Hispanic students, as compared to 10 percent in 1996.

Third, petitioner argues that considering race was not necessary because such consideration has had only a " 'minimal impact' in advancing the [University's] compelling interest." Again, the record does not support this assertion. In 2003, 11 percent of the Texas residents enrolled through holistic review were Hispanic and 3.5 percent were African-American. In 2007, by contrast, 16.9 percent of the Texas holistic-review freshmen were Hispanic and 6.8 percent were African-American. Those increases—of 54 percent and 94 percent, respectively—show that consideration of race has had a meaningful, if still limited, effect on the diversity of the University's freshman class. In any event, it is not a failure of narrow tailoring for the impact of racial consideration to be minor. The fact that race consciousness played a role in only a small portion of admissions decisions should be a hallmark of narrow tailoring, not evidence of unconstitutionality.

Petitioner's final argument is that "there are numerous other available race-neutral means of achieving" the University's compelling interest. A review of the record reveals, however, that, at the time of petitioner's application, none of her proposed alternatives was a workable means for the University to attain the benefits of diversity it sought. [In] the wake of *Hopwood*, the University spent seven years attempting to achieve its compelling interest using race-neutral holistic review. None of these efforts succeeded.

Petitioner suggests altering the weight given to academic and socioeconomic factors in the University's admissions calculus. This proposal ignores the fact that the University tried, and failed, to increase diversity through enhanced consideration of socioeconomic and other factors. And it further ignores this Court's precedent making clear that the Equal Protection Clause does not force universities to choose between a diverse student body and a reputation for academic excellence. *Grutter*.

Petitioner's final suggestion is to uncap the Top Ten Percent Plan, and admit more—if not all—the University's students through a percentage plan. As an initial matter, petitioner overlooks the fact that the Top Ten Percent Plan, though facially neutral, cannot be understood apart from its basic purpose, which is to boost minority enrollment. Percentage plans are "adopted with racially segregated neighborhoods and schools front and center stage." *Fisher I* (Ginsburg, J., dissenting). "It is race consciousness, not blindness to race, that drives such plans." Id. Consequently, petitioner cannot assert simply that increasing the University's reliance on a percentage plan would make its admissions policy more race neutral.

Even if, as a matter of raw numbers, minority enrollment would increase under such a regime, petitioner would be hard-pressed to find convincing support for the proposition that college admissions would be improved if they were a function of class rank alone. That approach would sacrifice all other aspects of diversity in pursuit of enrolling a higher number of minority students. [To] compel universities to admit students based on class rank alone is in deep tension with the goal of educational diversity as this Court's cases have defined it. *See Grutter.* At its center, the Top Ten Percent Plan is a blunt instrument that may well compromise the University's own definition of the diversity it seeks. * * *

The Court's affirmance of the University's admissions policy today does not necessarily mean the University may rely on that same policy without refinement. It is the University's ongoing obligation to engage in constant deliberation and continued reflection regarding its admissions policies.

JUSTICE KAGAN took no part in the consideration or decision of this case.

JUSTICE THOMAS, dissenting.

I join Justice Alito's dissent. [I] write separately to reaffirm that "a State's use of race in higher education admissions is categorically prohibited by the Equal Protection Clause." *Fisher I* (Thomas, J., dissenting).

[In his concurring opinion in *Fisher I*, Thomas, J. wrote: "My view of the Constitution is the one advanced by the plaintiffs in *Brown*: '[N]o State has any authority under the equal-protection clause of the Fourteenth Amendment to use race as a factor in affording educational opportunities among its citizens.' [This] principle is neither new nor difficult to understand. In 1868, decades before *Plessy*, the Iowa Supreme Court held that schools may not discriminate against applicants based on their skin color. In *Clark v. Board of Directors*, 24 Iowa 266 (1868), a school denied admission to a student because she was black, and 'public sentiment [was] opposed to the intermingling of white and colored children in the same schools.' The Iowa Supreme Court rejected that flimsy justification, holding that 'all the youths are equal before the law, and there is no discretion vested in the board [or] elsewhere, to interfere with or disturb that equality.'[2]

["The] worst forms of racial discrimination in this Nation have always been accompanied by straight-faced representations that discrimination helped minorities. Slaveholders argued that slavery was a 'positive good' that civilized blacks and elevated them in every dimension of life. [A] century later, segregationists similarly asserted [that] separate schools protected black children from racist white students and teachers. [The] University's discrimination 'stamp[s] [blacks and Hispanics] with a badge of inferiority.' [Although] most blacks and Hispanics attending the

---

[2]　The decision was based on Iowa law, not the Fourteenth Amendment.

University were admitted without discrimination under the Top Ten Percent plan [no] one can distinguish those students from the ones whose race played a role in their admission."]

JUSTICE ALITO, with whom ROBERTS. C.J., and THOMAS, J., join, dissenting.

[In] 2000, UT announced that [as a result of the conjunction of the Top Ten Percent Plan with a supplemental race-neutral holistic policy,] its "enrollment levels for African American and Hispanic freshmen have returned to those of 1996, the year before the *Hopwood* decision prohibited the consideration of race in admissions policies. [By] 2004—the last year under the holistic, race-neutral AI/PAI system—UT's entering class was 4.5% African-American, 17.9% Asian-American, and 16.9% Hispanic. The 2004 entering class thus had a higher percentage of African-Americans, Asian-Americans, and Hispanics than the class that entered in 1996, when UT had last employed racial preferences. Notwithstanding these lauded results, UT leapt at the opportunity to reinsert race into the process [in the aftermath of *Grutter*]. UT purports to have later engaged in "almost a year of deliberations," but there is no evidence that the reintroduction of race into the admissions process was anything other than a foregone conclusion.

[Although] UT claims that race is but a "factor of a factor of a factor of a factor," UT acknowledges that "race is the only one of [its] holistic factors that appears on the cover of every application." [Notwithstanding] the omnipresence of racial classifications, UT claims that it keeps no record of how those classifications affect its process. [Accordingly], UT asserts that it has no idea which students were admitted as a result of its race-conscious system and which students would have been admitted under a race-neutral process.

[Because] UT has failed to define its interest in using racial preferences with clarity, [the] narrow tailoring inquiry is impossible, and UT cannot satisfy strict scrutiny. When UT adopted its challenged policy, it characterized its compelling interest as obtaining a " 'critical mass' " of underrepresented minorities. [But] to this day, UT has not explained in anything other than the vaguest terms what it means by "critical mass." In fact, UT argues that it need not identify any interest more specific than "securing the educational benefits of diversity." [This] intentionally imprecise interest is designed to insulate UT's program from meaningful judicial review. [Without] knowing in reasonably specific terms what critical mass is or how it can be measured, a reviewing court cannot conduct the requisite "careful judicial inquiry" into whether the use of race was " 'necessary.' " *Fisher I*. [The aims that the University has advanced] are laudable goals, but they are not concrete or precise, and they offer no limiting principle for the use of racial preferences. For instance, how will a court ever be able to determine whether stereotypes have been adequately destroyed? Or whether cross-racial understanding has been adequately achieved? [By] accepting these amorphous goals as sufficient for UT to carry its burden, the majority violates decades of precedent rejecting blind deference to government officials defending " 'inherently suspect' " classifications. *Miller v. Johnson*, 515 U.S. 900 (1995).

[Although] UT's primary argument is that it need not point to any interest more specific than "the educational benefits of diversity," it has—at various points in this litigation—identified four more specific goals. [First], both UT and the majority cite demographic data as evidence that African-American and Hispanic students are "underrepresented" at UT and that racial preferences are necessary to compensate for this underrepresentation. [To] the extent that UT is pursuing parity with Texas demographics, that is nothing more than "outright racial balancing," which this Court has time and again held "patently unconstitutional." *Fisher I.*

[The] other major explanation UT offered in the Proposal [to resume taking race into account in admissions] was its desire to promote classroom diversity. [UT] now equivocates, disclaiming any discrete interest in classroom diversity. [Nor] is there any indication that UT instructed admissions officers to search for African-American and Hispanic applicants who would fill particular gaps at the classroom level.

[While] both the majority and the Fifth Circuit rely on UT's classroom study, they completely ignore its finding that Hispanics are better represented than Asian-Americans in UT classrooms. In fact, they act almost as if Asian-American students do not exist. [The] District Court acknowledged the impact of UT's policy on Asian-American students [those of whom who are admitted through holistic review tend to have higher scores that whites, African-Americans, or Hispanics, but] it brushed aside this impact, concluding—astoundingly—that UT can pick and choose which racial and ethnic groups it would like to favor. [This] reasoning, which the majority implicitly accepts by blessing UT's reliance on the classroom study, places the Court on the "tortuous" path of "decid[ing] which races to favor." [By] accepting the classroom study as proof that UT satisfied strict scrutiny, the majority "move[s] us from 'separate but equal' to 'unequal but benign.' "

UT also alleges—and the majority embraces—an interest in avoiding "feelings of loneliness and isolation" among minority students. In support of this argument, they cite only demographic data and anecdotal statements by UT officials that some students (we are not told how many) feel "isolated." This vague interest cannot possibly satisfy strict scrutiny.

[Even] assuming UT is correct that, under *Grutter*, it need only cite a generic interest in the educational benefits of diversity, its plan still fails strict scrutiny because it is not narrowly tailored. "If a ' "nonracial approach [could] promote the substantial interest about as well and at tolerable administrative expense," ' then the university may not consider race." *Fisher I.* Here, there is no evidence that race-blind, holistic review would not achieve UT's goals at least "about as well" as UT's race-based policy. In addition, UT could have adopted other approaches to further its goals, such as intensifying its outreach efforts, uncapping the Top Ten Percent Law, or placing greater weight on socioeconomic factors.

[The] fact that UT's racial preferences are unnecessary to achieve its stated goals is further demonstrated by their minimal effect on UT's diversity. In 2004, when race was not a factor, 3.6% of non-Top Ten Percent Texas enrollees were African-American and 11.6% were Hispanic. It would stand to reason that at least the same percentages of African-American and Hispanic students would have been admitted through holistic review in 2008 even if race were not a factor. If that assumption is correct, then race was determinative for only 15 African-American students and 18 Hispanic students in 2008 (representing 0.2% and 0.3%, respectively, of the total enrolled first-time freshmen from Texas high schools).

[The] majority purports to agree with much of the above analysis. [Yet it] frames its analysis as if petitioner bears the burden of proof here. First, the Court [notes an] "evidentiary gap" [concerning the effect of the University's policies. This gap should be fatal.] Under strict scrutiny, UT was required to identify evidence that race-based admissions were necessary to achieve a compelling interest before it put them in place.

[Second], in an effort to excuse UT's lack of evidence, the Court argues that because "the University lacks any authority to alter the role of the Top Ten Percent Plan," "it similarly had no reason to keep extensive data on the Plan or the students admitted under it—particularly in the years before *Fisher I* clarified the stringency of the strict-scrutiny burden for a school that employs race-conscious review." But UT has long been aware that it bears the burden of justifying its racial discrimination under strict scrutiny. [The] majority's willingness to cite UT's "good faith" as the basis for excusing its failure to adduce evidence is particularly inappropriate in light of UT's well-documented absence of good faith.

[The] majority concludes that UT has met its heavy burden [of satisfying strict scrutiny]. This conclusion is remarkable—and remarkably wrong.

KAGAN, J., did not participate.

NOTES AND QUESTIONS

1. ***Standard of review.*** Should race-based classificatory schemes that aim to advantage previously disadvantaged minorities be evaluated under the same strict judicial scrutiny as other racial classifications? If so, on what basis is strict scrutiny justified?

(a) *History.* Consider Jed Rubenfeld, *Affirmative Action,* 107 Yale L.J. 427 (1997): "In July 1866, the Thirty-Ninth Congress [that] had just framed the Fourteenth Amendment [passed] a statute appropriating money [for] 'the relief of destitute colored women and children.' In 1867, the Fortieth Congress—the same body that was driving the Fourteenth Amendment down the throat of the bloody South—passed a statute providing money for [the] destitute 'colored' persons in the [the District of Columbia]. Year after year in the Civil War period [Congress] made special appropriations for [the] 'colored' soldiers and sailors of the Union Army. [What] do [these statutes] prove? Only that those who profess fealty to the 'original understanding' [cannot] categorically condemn color-based distribution of governmental benefits."[3] Compare the view of Lino Graglia, *Racially Discriminatory Admission to Public Institutions of Higher Education,* in *Constitutional Government in America* 255, 263 (Ronald K.L. Collins ed., 1980), that arguments such as this risk proving "too much": "It is equally clear that the Fourteenth Amendment was not intended to prohibit school segregation either."

(b) *Moral relevance and permissibility.* Is the relevant constitutional principle that government should not classify by race (a principle sometimes labeled the "colorblindness" or "antidiscrimination" principle)? Or is it that government should not use race as a basis to demean, suppress, or stigmatize (a principle sometimes called the "antisubordination" principle)? Reva B. Siegel, *Equality Talk: Antisubordination and Anticlassification Values in Constitutional Struggles over* Brown, 117 Harv.L.Rev. 1470 (2004), argues that *Brown v. Board of Education* was initially understood as predicated on the harmfulness of segregation to subordinated blacks and that it was not viewed as creating a general prohibition against race-based classifications. It was for this reason, she says, that "throughout the 1960s, courts repeatedly held that state and local governments could use race-specific measures to break down de facto segregation or 'racial imbalance' in the nation's public schools, even when there was no finding of a constitutional violation." But courts "began to respond differently when plaintiffs challenged new race-conscious measures designed to help integrate the nation's universities."

(c) *The (variable) strictness of strict scrutiny?* A number of commentators have questioned whether *Grutter* and *Austin* apply the same "strict scrutiny" to affirmative action that it applies to classifications that burden racial minorities. Recall that in *Bakke,* Brennan, White, Marshall, and Blackmun, JJ., argued for less searching judicial scrutiny of affirmative action

---

[3] See also Eric Schnapper, *Affirmative Action and the Legislative History of the Fourteenth Amendment,* 71 Va.L.Rev. 753 (1985). But see Michael B. Rappaport, *Originalism and the Colorblind Constitution,* 89 Notre Dame L.Rev. 71 (2013) (arguing that because the Fourteenth Amendment does not apply to the federal government, federal statutes from the Reconstruction era do not reliably indicate the Amendment's original understanding, and further arguing that federal statutes that appear to discriminate on the basis of race "do not upon examination necessarily turn out to do so").

than for racial classifications applied to disadvantage minorities. Did their view prevail in *Grutter*?[4]

2.   *Diversity.* What is the nature of the "diversity" in which educational institutions have a compelling interest?

(a)   *Changing conceptions?* Consider Siegel, note 1(b) supra: "*Grutter* does not simply incorporate Justice Powell's diversity rationale, [but rather] transforms the diversity rationale in the course of adopting it. [In] *Grutter*, diversity is no longer merely the state's interest in ensuring that the learning environment in institutions of higher education is populated by persons of divergent life experience; the opinion also explains the value of diversity as the value of an educated citizenry in a democratic society. As it does so, the opinion defines the state interest in achieving 'diversity' as an interest in ensuring that no group is excluded from participating in public life and thus relegated to an outsider, or second-class status, as well as an interest in cultivating the confidence of all citizens that they have the opportunity to serve in positions of national leadership."

(b)   *Diversity as distraction?* Consider Derrick Bell, *Diversity's Distractions*, 103 Colum.L.Rev. 1622 (2003): "For at least four reasons, the concept of diversity, far from a viable means of ensuring affirmative action in the admissions processes of colleges and graduate schools, is a serious distraction in the ongoing efforts to achieve racial justice: 1) Diversity enables courts and policymakers to avoid addressing directly the barriers of race and class that adversely affect so many applicants; 2) Diversity invites further litigation by offering a distinction without a real difference between those uses of race approved in college admissions programs, and those in other far more important affirmative action programs that the Court has rejected; 3) Diversity serves to give undeserved legitimacy to the heavy reliance on grades and test scores that privilege well-to-do, mainly white applicants; and 4) The tremendous attention directed at diversity programs diverts concern and resources from the serious barriers of poverty that exclude far more students from entering college than are likely to gain admission under an affirmative action program." Are these matters that should appropriately concern courts that are called upon to review challenges to affirmative action programs?

3.   *Individualized judgments and quotas.* Is there any practical distinction between (a) a separate, identified program for minority admissions, (b) a program in which racial background gets an applicant a certain number of points that contribute to an overall admissions score, and (c) a program in which racial background can be counted as a "plus," and those administering the program—in order to get the desired "diversity"—monitor the number of admittees who fall within relevant categories?

---

[4]   According to Adam Winkler, *Fatal in Theory and Strict in Fact: An Empirical Analysis of Strict Scrutiny in the Federal Courts*, 59 Vand.L.Rev. 793 (2006), an empirical study of strict scrutiny in both the Supreme Court and in the lower federal courts from 1990 through 2003 reveals a survival rate of slightly more than 30% in the lower federal courts and of 25% in the Supreme Court.

Consider Reva Siegel, *From Colorblindness to Antibalkanization: An Emerging Ground of Decision in Race Equality Cases,* 120 Yale L.J. 1278 (2011): "[T]he Justices at the center of the Court who have cast the deciding votes to uphold and limit race-conscious civil rights initiatives often explain their position in opinions concerned with threats to social cohesion. Justices reasoning from this antibalkanization perspective enforce the Equal Protection Clause with attention to the forms of estrangement that both racial stratification and practices of racial remediation may engender. [Because] Justices reasoning from an antibalkanization perspective understand that interventions promoting racial integration can become a locus of racial conflict, they insist that race-conscious interventions undertaken for compelling public-regarding purposes must nonetheless anticipate and endeavor to ameliorate race-conscious resentments[, for example by requiring individualized judgment and forbidding quotas]. Race-conscious resentments among the racially privileged matter because, if ignored, they may inhibit the amelioration of racial stratification and because these resentments may reflect displaced expressions of other forms of inequality."

Compare Cristina M. Rodríguez, *Against Individualized Consideration,* 83 Indiana L.J. 1405 (2008): "Contrary to [conventional] wisdom, it is crude, mechanical decision making that [best] restrains the state in its race consciousness [in implementing affirmative action. [By] giving state actors the power to consider how race relates to particular individuals and their potential contributions, we encourage the development of semi-official definitions of the category—the very sorts of definitions that produce stereotypical thinking and deny that the experiences of race or ethnicity differ from individual to individual. [A] second danger posed by the individualized model is [the] personal essay problem: individualized consideration demands that people perform their ethnicity for admissions officers, either through their personal statements or in entrance interviews. [T]hese tensions [demonstrate] how the rise of the diversity interest as the justification for affirmative action has moved [us] away from an honest approach to what should be the animating purposes of a civil rights agenda: combating discrimination and eliminating its effects."

Jim Chen, *Diversity in a Different Dimension: Evolutionary Theory and Affirmative Action's Destiny,* 59 Ohio St.L.J. 811 (1998), argues that the "diversity" sought by affirmative action, which exalts the significance of race and levels differences among racial minorities, "is in many ways the polar opposite of [genuine] diversity."

4. ***Educational affirmative action in practice.*** William G. Bowen & Derek Bok, *The Shape of the River: Long-Term Consequences of Considering Race in College and University Admissions* (1998), presents the results of the first comprehensive, long-term study of affirmative action in 28 academically selective colleges and universities (based on data involving more than 80,000 undergraduates who matriculated in 1951, 1976, and 1989). The authors' assessments are generally enthusiastic. Among their conclusions: (i) In 1989, blacks made up about 7% of the classes in the colleges that they sampled;

without affirmative action, the number of black entrants would have been between 2.1% and 3.6%. (ii) Although the black drop-out rate was 11% higher than that for whites, 75% of the blacks in the 1989 cohort graduated from their original institution, and 79% graduated from some college, within six years. (iii) Black graduates of the elite schools earned considerably more on average than black graduates of non-elite schools. (iv) Almost twice as many blacks as whites from the 1976 cohort participate in community service organizations.

For a sustained critique of the methodology and argumentation of *The Shape of the River*, see Abigail Thernstrom & Stephen Thernstrom, *Reflections on The Shape of the River*, 46 U.C.L.A. L.Rev. 1583 (1999). Among the Thernstroms' major arguments are that black students admitted under what they call "racial double standards" tend not to do as well academically as students admitted without regard to race; that admissions policies at elite institutions have little impact on the socio-economic fabric of African-American life; and that racial categorization perpetuates habits of mind antithetical to egalitarian ideals. Richard H. Sander, *A Systemic Analysis of Affirmative Action in American Law Schools*, 57 Stan.L.Rev. 367 (2004), similarly finds that black law students who are admitted on the basis of affirmative action "preferences" (as distinguished from black students admitted without such "preferences") tend to receive lower grades than their white classmates, to be more likely to drop out of law school, and to be less likely to pass the bar exam. Sander further contends that African-American students are widely "mismatched" with law schools for which they lack proper credentials; that they therefore tend to drop out and to fail the bar exam at disproportionately high rates; and that, if racial preferences did not exist, "the production of black lawyers would rise significantly [and] blacks as a whole would be significantly better off." Sander's analysis has triggered a number of critical replies, largely focused on his methodology, to which he has in turn replied. See, for example, the exchange in 57 Stan.L.Rev. 1807 et seq. (2005).

5. ***The alternative of class-based affirmative action.*** Would affirmative action based on class or economic background be fairer or more constitutionally acceptable than affirmative action based on race?[5]

(a) ***Class-based affirmative action and minorities.*** There are varying estimates of the extent to which class-based affirmative action would succeed in promoting racial diversity in higher education, for example, and many observers are quite pessimistic. See, e.g., Matthew N. Gaertner & Melissa Hart, *Considering Class: College Access and Diversity*, 7 Harv.L. & Pol'y Rev. 367 (2013) ("Even if universities [in providing class-based preferences] were to grant low-income students 'minority-size' boosts, racial diversity would plummet because minority status and poverty are not sufficiently correlated. These simulations have been reproduced in subsequent research, and their results are consistently confirmed."). An additional

---

[5] For affirmative arguments, see, e.g., Richard H. Sander, *Class in American Legal Education*, 88 Denv. U.L.Rev. 631 (2011); Richard D. Kahlenberg, *Class-Based Affirmative Action*, 84 Calif. L.Rev. 1037 (1996); see also Deborah C. Malamud, *Class-Based Affirmative Action: Lessons and Caveats,* 74 Tex. L. Rev. 1847 (1996).

consideration is that the African-American students currently attending elite institutions tend not to come from the poorest black families. See Bowen & Bok, supra, at 50.

(b) *Level of judicial scrutiny.* If a class-based affirmative action program is racially neutral on its face, but is implemented for the *purpose* of achieving a racially defined effect (i.e., heightened minority representation), should it be subjected to rational basis review or to strict judicial scrutiny? Under *Washington v. Davis*, a facially neutral statute adopted for the purpose of advantaging whites and disadvantaging racial minorities would trigger strict scrutiny. Should the converse also hold?

B. Employment and Government Contracts

P. 1464, at end of note 4:

In TEXAS DEP'T OF HOUSING AND COMMUNITY AFFAIRS v. INCLUSIVE COMMUNITIES PROJECT, INC., 135 S.Ct. 2507 (2015), which held that disparate impact claims are cognizable under the Fair Housing Act (FHA), the 5–4 majority, per KENNEDY, J., noted that "[r]emedial orders that impose racial targets or quotas might raise [difficult] constitutional questions" and also construed the FHA to give "leeway" to defendants to justify policies serving "valid interest[s]." But, subject to those limitations, Kennedy, J., did not question the constitutionality of statutory causes of action based on racially disparate impacts. ALITO, J., joined by Roberts, C.J., and Scalia and Thomas, JJ., dissented on statutory grounds. Thomas, J., also filed a separate dissent in which he suggested that a federal cause of action based on disparate impact would violate the Constitution.

3. DISCRIMINATIONS BASED ON GENDER

II. DIFFERENCES—REAL AND IMAGINED

P. 1506, after *Nguyen*:

SESSIONS v. MORALES-SANTANA, 137 S.Ct. 1678 (2017), invalidated a provision of the Immigration and Nationality Act that gave unmarried mothers who are U.S. citizens a preference over unmarried citizen fathers and even married citizen couples in passing on U.S. citizenship to children born outside the U.S. The provision conditioned the capacity to pass on citizenship to offspring born abroad on a citizen's having resided in the U.S. for a number of years, but fewer for unwed citizen mothers than for other citizen parents. GINSBURG, J., reasoned: "Prescribing one rule for mothers, another for fathers, [requires] an 'exceedingly persuasive justification.' [Moreover], the classification must substantially serve an important governmental interest *today*, for 'in interpreting the [e]qual [p]rotection [guarantee], [we have] recognized that new insights and societal understandings can reveal unjustified inequality

. . . that once passed unnoticed and unchallenged.' [No] 'important [governmental] interest' is served by laws grounded [in] the obsolescing view that 'unwed fathers [are] invariably less qualified and entitled than mothers' to take responsibility for nonmarital children. Overbroad generalizations of that order [have] a constraining impact, descriptive though they may be of the way many people still order their lives.[13] Laws according or denying benefits in reliance on '[s]tereotypes about women's domestic roles' [may] 'creat[e] a self-fulfilling cycle of discrimination that force[s] women to continue to assume the role of primary family caregiver.'

"[A] man needs no more time in the United States than a woman 'in order to have assimilated citizenship-related values to transmit to [his] child.' " The Court rejected the argument that because an "unwed mother [is] the child's only 'legally recognized' parent at the time of childbirth[, a] longer physical connection to the United States is warranted for the unwed father [to counteract] the 'competing national influence' of the alien mother. [One] cannot see in this driven-by-gender scheme the close means-end fit required to survive heightened scrutiny." The Government also argued that "[Congress] established the gender-based residency differential [in order to] reduce the risk that a foreign-born child of a U.S. citizen would be born stateless. [But] there is little reason to believe that a statelessness concern prompted the diverse physical-presence requirements. Nor has the Government shown that the risk of statelessness disproportionately endangered the children of unwed mothers."

Ginsburg, J., distinguished *Nguyen* on the ground that it involved the legitimacy of a "paternal-acknowledgment requirement on fathers" as a means of establishing "a biological parent-child relationship" that the Government did not dispute.[6]

---

[13] [Ct's Note] "Even if stereotypes frozen into legislation have 'statistical support,' our decisions reject measures that classify unnecessarily and overbroadly by gender when more accurate and impartial lines can be drawn."

[6] Despite having ruled the challenged statute invalid, the Court found that it could not order a conferral of citizenship on Morales-Santana because "Congress likely would have chosen [a different remedy] 'had it been apprised' " of the equal protection violation in its discriminatory scheme: rather than turn a narrow exception for unwed mothers into the general rule, Congress likely would have achieved equality by subjecting unwed citizen mothers to the same U.S. residency requirements as unwed citizen fathers and married couples before they could pass on their citizenship to children born abroad. Thomas, J., joined by Alito, J., concurred only in the judgment, believing that because the Court could not award relief in any event, it should not have reached the merits of the equal protection issue. Gorsuch, J., took no part.

4. SPECIAL SCRUTINY FOR OTHER CLASSIFICATIONS: DOCTRINE AND DEBATES

I. SEXUAL ORIENTATION

P. 1523, substitute for *United States v. Windsor* and Notes and Questions that follow:

In UNITED STATES v. WINDSOR, 133 S.Ct. 2675 (2013), the Court, per KENNEDY, J., invalidated a provision of the Defense of Marriage Act (DOMA) that denied federal recognition to same-sex marriages authorized by state law: "[By] history and tradition the definition and regulation of marriage [have] been treated as being within the authority and realm of the separate States. [The challenged provision's] operation is directed to a class of persons that the laws of New York, and of 11 other States, have sought to protect. [DOMA] rejects the long established precept that the incidents, benefits, and obligations of marriage are uniform for all married couples within each State, though they may vary, subject to constitutional guarantees, from one State to the next. [DOMA] seeks to injure the very class New York seeks to protect. By doing so it violates basic due process and equal protection principles applicable to the Federal Government. See U.S. Const., Amdt. 5; *Bolling* v. *Sharpe*. The Constitution's guarantee of equality 'must at the very least mean that a bare congressional desire to harm a politically unpopular group cannot' justify disparate treatment of that group. In determining whether a law is motivated by an improper animus or purpose, '[d]iscriminations of an unusual character' especially require careful consideration. DOMA cannot survive under these principles. DOMA's unusual deviation from the usual tradition of recognizing and accepting state definitions of marriage here operates to deprive same-sex couples of the benefits and responsibilities that come with the federal recognition of their marriages. This is strong evidence of a law having the purpose and effect of disapproval of that class. The avowed purpose and practical effect of the law here in question are to impose a disadvantage, a separate status, and so a stigma upon all who enter into same-sex marriages made lawful by the unquestioned authority of the States.

"The principal purpose is to impose inequality, not for other reasons like governmental efficiency. [DOMA] undermines both the public and private significance of state sanctioned same-sex marriages; for it tells those couples, and all the world, that their otherwise valid marriages are unworthy of federal recognition. This places same-sex couples in an unstable position of being in a second-tier marriage. The differentiation demeans the couple, whose moral and sexual choices the Constitution protects, see *Lawrence*, and whose relationship the State has sought to dignify. And it humiliates tens of thousands of children now being raised by same-sex couples."

ROBERTS, C.J., dissented: "Interests in uniformity and stability amply justified Congress's decision to retain the definition of marriage that, [when DOMA was enacted in 1996], had been adopted by every State in our Nation, and every nation in the world."

SCALIA, J., joined by Thomas, J., and in part by Roberts, C.J., also dissented: "[The] opinion starts with seven full pages about the traditional power of States to define domestic relations[, but] we are eventually told that 'it is unnecessary to decide whether this federal intrusion on state power is a violation of the Constitution.' [If] this is meant to be an equal-protection opinion, it is a confusing one. The opinion does not resolve and indeed does not even mention what had been the central question in this litigation: whether, under the Equal Protection Clause, laws restricting marriage to a man and a woman are reviewed for more than mere rationality. [As] nearly as I can tell, the Court [does] not apply strict scrutiny, and its central propositions are taken from rational-basis cases like *Moreno*. But the Court certainly does not *apply* anything that resembles that deferential framework.

"[The] sum of all the Court's nonspecific hand-waving is that this law is invalid because it is motivated by a 'bare . . . desire to harm' couples in same-sex marriages. [But] there are many perfectly valid—indeed, downright boring—justifying rationales for this legislation. [To] choose just one[,] DOMA avoids difficult choice-of-law issues that will now arise absent a uniform federal definition of marriage. Imagine a pair of women who marry in Albany and then move to Alabama, which does not 'recognize as valid any marriage of parties of the same sex.' When the couple files their next federal tax return, may it be a joint one? Which State's law controls, for federal-law purposes: their State of celebration (which recognizes the marriage) or their State of domicile (which does not)? [The] Court mentions none of this. Instead, it accuses the Congress that enacted this law and the President who signed it of [having] acted with *malice*—with the *'purpose'* 'to disparage and to injure' same-sex couples. * * * I am sure these accusations are quite untrue.

"[T]he view that *this* Court will take of state prohibition of same-sex marriage is indicated beyond mistaking by today's opinion. [By] formally declaring anyone opposed to same-sex marriage an enemy of human decency, the majority arms well every challenger to a state law restricting marriage to its traditional definition."

Alito, J., joined in part by Thomas, J., also dissented.

———

In OBERGEFELL v. HODGES, 135 S.Ct. 2584 (2015), p. 27 of this Supplement, the Court, again per KENNEDY, J., held that the Fourteenth Amendment creates a fundamental liberty right encompassing same-sex marriage. After finding a right of same-sex couples to marry under the Due Process Clause: "The right of same-sex couples to marry that is part of the liberty promised by the Fourteenth Amendment is derived, too, from that Amendment's guarantee of the equal protection of the laws. The Due Process Clause and the Equal Protection Clause are connected in a profound way, though they set forth independent principles. [In] any particular case one Clause may be thought to capture the essence of the right in a more accurate and comprehensive way, even as the two Clauses may converge in the identification and definition of the right. [The] Court's cases touching upon the right to marry reflect this dynamic. In *Loving* the Court invalidated a prohibition on interracial marriage under both the Equal Protection Clause and the Due Process Clause. The Court first declared the prohibition invalid because of its unequal treatment of interracial couples. It stated: 'There can be no doubt that restricting the freedom to marry solely because of racial classifications violates the central meaning of the Equal Protection Clause.' With this link to equal protection the Court proceeded to hold the prohibition offended central precepts of liberty: 'To deny this fundamental freedom on so unsupportable a basis as the racial classifications embodied in these statutes, classifications so directly subversive of the principle of equality at the heart of the Fourteenth Amendment, is surely to deprive all the State's citizens of liberty without due process of law.' The reasons why marriage is a fundamental right became more clear and compelling from a full awareness and understanding of the hurt that resulted from laws barring interracial unions.

"[It] is now clear that the challenged laws burden the liberty of same-sex couples, and it must be further acknowledged that they abridge central precepts of equality. Here the marriage laws enforced by the respondents are in essence unequal: same-sex couples are denied all the benefits afforded to opposite-sex couples and are barred from exercising a fundamental right. Especially against a long history of disapproval of their relationships, this denial to same-sex couples of the right to marry works a grave and continuing harm. The imposition of this disability on gays and lesbians serves to disrespect and subordinate them. And the Equal Protection Clause, like the Due Process Clause, prohibits this unjustified infringement of the fundamental right to marry."

ROBERTS, C.J., joined by Scalia and Thomas, JJ., dissented: "[The] marriage laws at issue here do not violate the Equal Protection Clause, because distinguishing between opposite-sex and same-sex couples is rationally related to the States' 'legitimate state interest' in 'preserving the traditional institution of marriage' [as a union of one man and one woman that 'arose in the nature of things to meet a vital need: ensuring that children are conceived by a mother and father committed to raising them in the stable conditions of a lifelong relationship.'] It is important to note with precision which laws petitioners have challenged. Although they discuss some of the ancillary legal benefits that accompany marriage, such as hospital visitation rights and recognition of spousal status on official documents, petitioners' lawsuits target the laws defining marriage generally rather than those allocating benefits specifically. The equal protection analysis might be different, in my view, if we were confronted with a more focused challenge to the denial of certain tangible benefits."

Scalia, J., Thomas, J., and Alito, J., also filed dissenting opinions.

NOTES AND QUESTIONS

1. ***Equal protection and due process.*** Does the equal protection discussion in *Obergefell* add anything to the Court's due process analysis? If not, why did the Court include it?

2. ***Standard of review.*** The holding in *Obergefell* rests heavily on the premise that marriage is a fundamental right, any restriction on which would trigger searching judicial scrutiny under well-established equal protection principles. See Sec. 5 of this Chapter (discussing fundamental rights under the Equal Protection Clause). What implications does the decision have for possible discriminations against gays not involving fundamental rights? Are all such discriminations motivated by animus or otherwise irrational?

5. FUNDAMENTAL RIGHTS

I. VOTING

B. "Dilution" of the Right: Apportionment

P. 1565, at end of note 3:

Harris v. Ariz. Ind. Redistricting Comm'n, 136 S.Ct. 1301 (2016), held that where "the maximum population deviation between the largest and the smallest [state legislative] district[s] [was] less than 10%, the [challengers could not] simply rely upon the numbers to show" a constitutional violation. Instead, they would have had to prove it was "more probable than not that illegitimate considerations [such as a wish to achieve partisan advantage] were the predominant motivation behind [deviations] that were under 10%."

P. 1566, at end of note 4:

In EVENWEL v. ABBOTT, 136 S.Ct. 1120 (2016), the Court, by 8–0, rejected an argument that principles barring vote dilution under the Equal Protection Clause require states to use numbers of eligible voters, rather than total population, as the basis for apportioning state legislative districts.

Writing for six Justices, Ginsburg, J., held that "constitutional history, this Court's decisions, and longstanding practice" all supported the conclusion that a "[s]tate may draw its legislative districts based on total population." She also noted that a Senator explaining the meaning of Section Two of the Fourteenth Amendment in a debate on the Senate floor had said " 'Numbers, not voters; numbers, not property; this is the theory of the Constitution.' " The plaintiffs, she continued, argued for "a rule inconsistent with this 'theory of the Constitution.' " Nevertheless, the Court reserved the question whether a state that so chose "may draw districts to equalize voter-eligible population rather than total population." Thomas and Alito, JJ., concurring in the judgment only, both distanced themselves from any intimation that the Constitution might require, rather than permit, states to use total populations as their base in drawing state legislative districts.

C. "Dilution" of the Right: Partisan Gerrymanders

P. 1575, at end of second paragraph of note 2:

In ARIZONA STATE LEGISLATURE v. ARIZONA INDEPENDENT REDISTRICTING COMM'N, 135 S.Ct. 2652 (2015), the Court, per Ginsburg, J. upheld a state ballot proposition that removed redistricting authority from the legislature and vested it in an independent commission. No one doubted that the state could provide for the drawing of districts for seats in the state legislature by a nonpartisan commission, and the Court, by 5 to 4, rejected a challenge to the commission's authority to redraw congressional districts under Art. I, sec. 4, cl. 1, which provides that "The Times, Places, and Manner of holding Elections for Senators and Representatives, shall be prescribed in each State by the Legislature thereof; but the Congress may at any time by Law make or alter such Regulations": "The dominant purpose of the Elections Clause [was] to empower Congress to override state election rules, not to restrict the way States enact legislation," including legislation establishing an independent redistricting commission. In support of that conclusion, Ginsburg, J., cited Founding-era dictionaries that defined "legislature" as "[t]he power that makes laws." She also quoted precedent asserting that "[t]he meaning of the word 'legislature,' used several times in the Federal Constitution, differs according to the connection in which it is employed" and noted that "[the] Court has 'long recognized the role of the States as laboratories for devising solutions to difficult legal problems.' "

ROBERTS, C.J., joined by Scalia, Thomas and Alito, JJ., dissented: "The Constitution includes seventeen provisions referring to a State's 'Legislature.' Every one [is] consistent with the understanding of a legislature as a representative body" and "many [are] flatly incompatible with the majority's reading of 'the Legislature' to refer to the people as a whole. [For] better or worse, the Elections Clause [does] not allow [Arizona voters] to address [their] concerns [about partisan redistricting] by displacing their legislature." Roberts, C.J., emphasized that it had taken the Seventeenth Amendment to transfer power to elect Senators from state legislatures to the voters. He concluded that Arizonans who disliked having the legislature redraw congressional districts could either "seek relief from Congress, which can [alter] the regulations prescribed by the legislature [or] follow the lead of the reformers who won passage of the Seventeenth Amendment."

D. "Dilution" of the Right: Issues Involving Race

P. 1594, substitute for *Bush v. Vera* and the Notes and Questions that follow on pages 1594–1598:

COOPER V. HARRIS
___ U.S. ___, 137 S.Ct. 1455, ___ L.Ed.2d ___ (2017).

JUSTICE KAGAN delivered the opinion of the Court.

The Equal Protection Clause of the Fourteenth Amendment [prevents] a State, in the absence of "sufficient justification," from "separating its citizens into different voting districts on the basis of race." When a voter sues state officials for drawing such race-based lines, our decisions call for a two-step analysis. First, the plaintiff must prove that "race was the predominant factor motivating the legislature's decision to place a significant number of voters within or without a particular district." *Miller v. Johnson*.[1] [Second,] if racial considerations predominated over others, [the] burden thus shifts to the State to prove that its race-based sorting of voters serves a "compelling interest" and is "narrowly tailored" to that end.

This Court has long assumed that one compelling interest is complying with operative provisions of the Voting Rights Act of 1965 (VRA or Act). Two provisions of the VRA—§ 2 and § 5—are involved in this case. Section 2 prohibits "vote dilution"—brought about, most relevantly here, by the "dispersal of [a group's members] into districts in which they constitute an ineffective minority of voters." *Thornburg v. Gingles*. Section 5, [before] *Shelby County v. Holder*, [required various] North Carolina counties to pre-clear voting changes with the Department of Justice, so as to forestall "retrogression" in the ability of racial minorities to elect their preferred candidates.

This case concerns North Carolina's most recent redrawing of two congressional districts, both of which have long included substantial populations of black voters. Both have quite the history before this Court[, beginning] in *Shaw v. Reno*, [which] held [that the predecessors of the same districts challenged in this case, Districts 1 and 12] were unwarranted racial gerrymanders. [After *Shaw*,] the State responded with a new districting plan[, and the Court upheld] a new District 12. See *Hunt v. Cromartie*, 526 U. S. 541 (1999) (*Cromartie I*); *Easley v. Cromartie*, 532 U.

---

[1] [Ct's Note] A plaintiff succeeds at this stage even if the evidence reveals that a legislature elevated race to the predominant criterion in order to advance other goals, including political ones.

S. 234 (2001) (*Cromartie II*). Racial considerations, we held, did not predominate in designing the revised District 12. Rather, that district was the result of a political gerrymander—[a constitutionally permissible] effort to engineer, mostly "without regard to race," a safe Democratic seat.

Another census, in 2010, necessitated [the] congressional map [at] issue in this case. State Senator Robert Rucho and State Representative David Lewis, both Republicans, chaired the two committees jointly responsible for preparing the revamped plan. They hired Dr. Thomas Hofeller, a veteran political mapmaker, to assist them in redrawing district lines. [After the] 2010 census had revealed District 1 to be substantially underpopulated, [the] State needed to place almost 100,000 new people within the district's boundaries. Rucho, Lewis, and Hofeller chose to take most of those people from heavily black areas of Durham, requiring a finger-like extension of the district's western line. With that addition, District 1's [black voting-age population or] BVAP rose from 48.6% to 52.7%. [Although] District 12 [had] no need for significant total-population changes, Rucho, Lewis, and Hofeller decided to reconfigure the district, further narrowing its already snakelike body while adding areas at either end. [As] the district gained some 35,000 African-Americans of voting age and lost some 50,000 whites of that age, its BVAP increased from 43.8% to 50.7%. After a bench trial, a three-judge District Court [ruled] that racial considerations predominated in the design of [both Districts 1 and 12 and that both were constitutionally invalid].

[With regard to District 1, uncontested] evidence [shows] that the State's mapmakers [purposefully] established a racial target [as the predominant factor in their revisions[3]]: African-Americans should make up no less than a majority of the voting-age population[.] [The] more substantial question is whether District 1 can survive the strict scrutiny applied to racial gerrymanders. [The State argues that it] had "good reasons to believe it needed to draw [District 1] as a majority-minority district to avoid Section 2 liability" for vote dilution. [But] electoral history provided no evidence that a § 2 plaintiff could demonstrate the third *Gingles* prerequisite [in addition to the requirements that a minority community be large and compact enough to constitute a district-wide majority and that it be politically cohesive]—effective white bloc-voting. For most of the twenty years prior to the new plan's adoption, African-Americans had made up less than a majority of District 1's voters; the district's BVAP usually hovered between 46% and 48%. Yet throughout

---

[3] **[Ct's Note]** The State's argument to the contrary rests on a legal proposition that [racial] considerations cannot predominate in drawing district lines unless there is an "actual conflict" between those lines and "traditional districting principles." But we rejected that view earlier this Term, holding that when (as here) race furnished "the overriding reason for choosing one map over others," a further showing of "inconsistency between the enacted plan and traditional redistricting criteria" is unnecessary to a finding of racial predominance. *Bethune-Hill v. Virginia State Bd. of Elections*, 137 S.Ct. 788 (2017).

those two decades, as the District Court noted, District 1 was "an extraordinarily safe district for African-American preferred candidates." [In] the lingo of voting law, District 1 functioned [as] a "crossover" district, in which members of the majority help a "large enough" minority to elect its candidate of choice. [Because] this Court has made clear that unless each of the three *Gingles* prerequisites is established, "there neither has been a wrong nor can be a remedy," [the challenge to District 1 must be upheld].

[The legality of District 12] turns solely on which of two possible reasons predominantly explains its most recent reconfiguration[—race or Republican political advantage]. [Because] "racial identification is highly correlated with political affiliation," [a trial court] must make "a sensitive inquiry" into all "circumstantial and direct evidence of intent" to assess whether the plaintiffs have managed to disentangle race from politics and prove that the former drove a district's lines.[7] Our job is different—and generally easier. [W]e review a district court's finding as to racial predominance only for clear error, except when the court made a legal mistake.

[By further slimming a district in which no substantial population changes were necessary] (and adding a couple of knobs to its snakelike body), [the] General Assembly incorporated tens of thousands of new voters and pushed out tens of thousands of old ones. And those changes followed racial lines. [The] Assembly thus turned District 12 [into] a majority-minority district. Rucho and Lewis had publicly stated that racial considerations lay behind District 12's augmented BVAP. In a release issued along with their draft districting plan, the two legislators ascribed that change to the need to achieve preclearance of the plan under § 5 of the VRA.

[The] State's contrary story—that politics alone drove decisionmaking—came into the trial mostly through Hofeller's testimony. Hofeller explained that Rucho and Lewis instructed him, first and foremost, to make the map as a whole "more favorable to Republican candidates." [The] District Court, however, disbelieved Hofeller's asserted indifference to the new district's racial composition.

[The] State mounts a final, legal rather than factual, attack on the District Court's finding of racial predominance. When race and politics are competing explanations of a district's lines, argues North Carolina, [quoting *Cromartie II*,] the party challenging the district must [introduce]

---

[7] [**Ct's Note**] As earlier noted, that inquiry is satisfied when legislators have "place[d] a significant number of voters within or without" a district predominantly because of their race, regardless of [whether they] use race as their predominant districting criterion with the end goal of advancing their partisan interests. [In] other words, the sorting of voters on the grounds of their race remains suspect even if race is meant to function as a proxy for other (including political) characteristics.

"an alternative [map] that achieves the legislature's political objectives while improving racial balance." [We] have no doubt that an alternative districting plan, of the kind North Carolina describes, can serve as key evidence in a race-versus-politics dispute. But in no area of our equal protection law have we forced plaintiffs to submit one particular form of proof to prevail.

THOMAS, J., concurring.

I join the opinion of the Court because it correctly applies our precedents [and] represents a welcome course correction to this Court's [previously insufficiently deferential] application of the clear-error standard.

ALITO, J., joined by ROBERTS, C.J., and KENNEDY, J., concurring in the judgment in part and dissenting in part.

[I concur in the judgment of the Court regarding Congressional District 1. The State concedes that the district was intentionally created as a majority-minority districts. And appellants have not satisfied strict scrutiny.]

[District 12 is governed by the rule of *Cromartie II*, under which] "the party attacking the legislatively drawn boundaries must show at the least that the legislature could have achieved its legitimate political objectives in alternative ways that are comparably consistent with traditional districting principles [and] that those districting alternatives would have brought about significantly greater racial balance."

[C]ourts are obligated to "exercise extraordinary caution in adjudicating claims that a State has drawn district lines on the basis of race." [As] we have acknowledged, "[p]olitics and political considerations are inseparable from districting and apportionment," and it is well known that state legislative majorities very often attempt to gain an electoral advantage through that process. See *Davis v. Bandemer*. [W]hile some might find [the result] distasteful, "[o]ur prior decisions have made clear that a jurisdiction may engage in constitutional political gerrymandering, even if it so happens that the most loyal Democrats happen to be black Democrats and even if the State were conscious of that fact." *Cromartie I*. [And if] around 90% of African-American voters cast their ballots for the Democratic candidate, as they have in recent elections, a plan that packs Democratic voters will look very much like a plan[ ] that packs African-American voters.

[*Cromartie II*'s rule that challengers] must submit an alternative map demonstrating that the legislature could have achieved its political goals without the racial effects giving rise to the racial gerrymandering allegation [should be applied in this case]. [When] a federal court says that race was a legislature's predominant purpose in drawing a district, it accuses the legislature of "offensive and demeaning" conduct. [That] is a grave accusation. [In] addition, "[f]ederal-court review of districting legislation represents a serious intrusion on the most vital of local functions" because "[i]t is well settled that reapportionment is primarily the duty and responsibility of the State." [Finally, unless] courts "exercise extraordinary caution" in distinguishing race-based redistricting from politics-based redistricting, they will invite the losers in the redistricting process to seek to obtain in court what they could not achieve in the political arena.

Even if we set aside the challengers' failure to submit an alternative map, the District Court's finding that race predominated in the drawing of District 12 is clearly erroneous. The State offered strong and coherent evidence that politics, not race, was the legislature's predominant aim, and the evidence supporting the District Court's contrary finding is weak.[7]

The basic shape of District 12 was legitimately taken as a given. Dr. Hofeller began with the prior version of District 12 [and, he testified,] moved more Democratic voters into District 12 in order to "increase Republican opportunities in the surrounding districts." [The] results of subsequent congressional elections show that Dr. Hofeller's plan achieved its goal.[8]

---

[7] In response to this line of argument, the majority countered: "[The] dissent repeatedly flips the appropriate standard of review. [It] mistakes the rule that a legislature's good faith should be presumed 'until a claimant makes a showing sufficient to support th[e] allegation' of 'race-based decisionmaking' for a kind of super-charged, pro-State presumption on appeal, trumping clear-error review." The dissent in turn replied: "Because the evidence [the plaintiffs] put forward is so weak, they have failed to carry [their] burden, and it was clear error for the District Court to hold otherwise."

[8] In *North Carolina v. Covington*, 137 S.Ct. 1624 (2017), the Court summarily affirmed a ruling that 28 majority-black state legislative districts were unconstitutional racial gerrymanders. But the Court, *per curiam*, vacated aspects of the district court's remedial order that shortened the terms of legislators who were elected in affected districts to one year and mandated special elections to fill seats from replacement districts. The district court's cursory balancing of the equities "would appear to justify a special election in *every* racial gerrymandering case." Emphasizing the need for "careful case-specific analysis," the Court remanded the case with instructions to weigh "considerations includ[ing] the severity and nature of the particular constitutional violation, the extent of the likely disruption to the ordinary processes of governance if early elections are imposed, and the need to act with proper judicial restraint when intruding on state sovereignty." The Court's brief opinion did "not suggest anything about the relative weight of these factors (or others)."

CHAPTER 12

LIMITATIONS ON JUDICIAL POWER AND REVIEW

■ ■ ■

2. STANDING

II. CONGRESSIONAL POWER TO CREATE STANDING

P. 1782, at end of note 2:

In SPOKEO, INC. v. ROBINS, 136 S.Ct. 1540 (2016), the Court, per ALITO, J., reaffirmed that "Congress may 'elevat[e] to the status of legally cognizable injuries concrete, *de facto* injuries that were previously inadequate in law.'" But Alito, J., also emphasized once again that "Congress' role in identifying and elevating intangible harms does not mean that a plaintiff automatically satisfies the injury-in-fact requirement whenever a statute grants a person a statutory right and purports to authorize that person to sue to vindicate that right." To satisfy Article III, the plaintiff must allege an injury that is both "particularized" and "concrete," Alito, J., affirmed.

Spokeo involved a dispute under the Fair Credit Reporting Act, which requires "fair and accurate credit reporting" and provides a statutory cause of action against "[a]ny person who willfully fails to comply with" its requirements. Robins brought suit against Spokeo, a "people search engine," which falsely reported, inter alia, that he was married, had a graduate degree, and was economically well off, when in fact he was out of work and seeking employment.

Alito, J.'s, opinion recognized that Robins had alleged an injury particularized to him, but noted that "not all inaccuracies cause harm or present any material risk of harm," as illustrated by the example of the dissemination of an incorrect zip code. Having distinguished the particularity and concreteness inquiries, Alito, J., concluded that the lower court had failed to analyze "whether the particular procedural violations alleged in this case entail a degree of risk sufficient to meet the concreteness requirement." In light of this analytical defect, the Court remanded the case for further proceedings without deciding whether Robins "adequately alleged an injury in fact."

GINSBURG, J., joined by Sotomayor, J., dissented. Although Ginsburg, J., "agree[d] with much of the Court's opinion," she would have affirmed the lower court's decision to uphold standing without a remand, based on the allegation in Robins' complaint that "Spokeo's misinformation 'cause[s] actual harm to [his] employment prospects.'"

III. TAXPAYER STANDING AND OTHER STATUS-BASED STANDING ISSUES

P. 1790, at end of note 5(b):

(c)   In ARIZONA STATE LEGISLATURE v. ARIZONA INDEPENDENT REDISTRICTING COMM'N, 135 S.Ct. 2652 (2015), p. 115 of this Supplement, the Court, per GINSBURG, J., upheld the standing of the Arizona Legislature to challenge the constitutionality of a ballot proposition that removed redistricting authority from the legislature and vested it in an independent commission: "The Arizona Legislature [is] an institutional plaintiff asserting an institutional injury, [which] commenced this action after authorizing votes in both of its chambers." The injury was concrete because "Proposition 106, together with the Arizona Constitution's ban on efforts to undermine the purposes of an initiative, would 'completely nullif[y]' any vote by the Legislature [purporting] to adopt a redistricting plan." The Court added in a footnote: "The case before us does not [concern] whether Congress has standing to bring a suit against the President. [Such] a suit [would] raise separation-of-powers concerns absent here." SCALIA, J., joined by Thomas, J., dissented with respect to standing as well as the merits: "[H]istory and judicial tradition show [that] courts do not resolve direct disputes between two political branches of the same government regarding their respective powers." (Roberts, C.J., dissented with respect to the merits only in an opinion joined by Scalia, Thomas, and Alito, JJ.)